Simple Sermons
on the
Christian Life

Simple Sermons
on the
Christian Life

by
W. HERSCHEL FORD, B.A., D.D.

ZONDERVAN PUBLISHING HOUSE
GRAND RAPIDS, MICHIGAN

But if we [really] are living *and* walking in the Light as He [Himself] is in the Light, we have (true, unbroken) fellowship with one another, and the blood of Jesus *Christ* His Son cleanses (removes) us from all sin *and* guilt — keeps us cleansed from sin in all its forms *and* manifestations.

I John 1:7 *(Amplified New Testament)*

Contents

Simple Sermons
on the
Christian Life

1.

The Christian's Love Life
John 21:15-17

Dr. Frank Patterson tells the story of a young pastor and his wife whom everyone loved very much. They had a dear little son named Robert, who was the idol of all the church members. Then Robert became sick and died and many hearts were broken. Some weeks later the young preacher came to the pulpit and brought with him some of the things which belonged to Robert. He brought a pair of little shoes and a little red wagon. He said to his congregation, "As we go through the house everything reminds us of Robert. We love these little shoes and this little wagon, not for themselves, but because Robert loved them." Then he made the application, stating that we ought to love the things which Jesus loved.

If we love people we cannot help but love the things that they love. If we love Jesus we will love that which He loved and give our lives to the things for which He died. One day He tested Peter in this way. Peter and the disciples had been fishing all night. When the morning came they saw the risen Christ on the shore. Peter did not wait for the boat to take him to the shore but threw himself into the water and came as quickly as he could. Jesus knew that the disciples would be hungry, so He had a fire ready and fish and bread prepared for them. After they had eaten breakfast together, Jesus turned to Peter and said, "Lovest thou Me?" Three times Jesus asked this question. Peter replied, "Lord, Thou knowest all things, Thou knowest that I love Thee." Then Jesus said, in effect, "Then show your love by giving your life to the things which I love." Did Peter do this? Yes, he became the

13

preacher at Pentecost and spent the rest of his life serving Christ, dying at last for His sake. He loved Jesus, therefore he loved the things which Jesus loved.

I want to ask you a question. Do you love the things which Jesus loved? You do if you love Jesus. Let me mention some of these things.

I. JESUS LOVED THE HEAVENLY FATHER — SO SHOULD WE

One day a lawyer asked Him the question, "What is the greatest commandment?" And Jesus replied, "To love the Heavenly Father with all the heart, soul and mind." Oh, how Jesus loved Him! He loved Him before the world began. He loved Him when God said, "Let us make man in our own image." He loved Him down through the ages. He loved Him when He had to leave home and come into the world to die for lost men. He loved Him in the Garden of Gethsemane when He said, "Not my will but Thine be done." He loved Him on the cross when He cried out, "My God, My God, why hast Thou forsaken Me?" He must have been homesick for heaven all the time that He was on earth. Surely He was glad when the hour came that He could go home and be with the Heavenly Father once again.

Jesus loved the Father. Do you? Before you were born God loved you. When you were in sin God gave His Only Begotten Son because He loved you. He sent His Spirit to convict you of sin and He saved you and wrote your name on high because He loved you. He has blessed you over the years by giving you health and home and loved ones and friends. "Every good gift and every perfect gift cometh down from the Father." Yes, you have made good. You have built your business, you have bought a home, you have worked hard for all that you have. But who is behind it all? Who gave you the strength to work? God did it all. He loves you. How much do you love Him?

My father had a hard life, for we were very poor. I am sure that I hurt him because of my sin. But later on I was converted and called to preach. He was proud of that fact and he would often say to other preachers, "Do you know my preacher boy?" When I would go anywhere near the old home and preach he would come and sit in the congregation and weep. I tried in his latter years to be a good son, but I wish I had done more to ease his many burdens. He died one June day and now I wish that I had been a better son. My friends, God loves you. You have hurt His heart with your sin. He rejoiced when you turned away from your sin and came to Him. Don't you think you ought to be a better child of God? Jesus loved the Heavenly Father. Shouldn't you love Him more?

II. JESUS LOVED THE WORD OF GOD — SO SHOULD WE

If we love the Father, surely we will love His Word. If a boy loves a girl he loves every word that she says. We know that Jesus loved the Word, because He quoted it often. He told of its imperishable character. He said that heaven and earth would pass away, but that God's Word would live forever. To Jesus the Bible was a letter from home, His heavenly home. He loved the Word.

Do you love the Bible? Oh yes, you own one. When you were converted you bought a new Bible and you were very proud of it. But what did you do with it? You took it home and put it on the table where everyone could see it, but you never use it. When you buy a car you use that car. When you buy a suit or television set you use them. Yet you buy a Bible, the Word of God to your heart, but you never open it, you never read it, you never use it. Is that the sensible thing to do?

If you want to know about God you must go to the Bible. If you want to know about Christ and salvation, go to the Bible. If you want to know the way to live and what church to join and how much to give, you go to the Bible. If you want to know about heaven and hell and Christ's Second Coming, you go to the Bible. It is a whole library in one volume. All the wisdom of earth is packed into its pages. If I could pay the highest tribute ever paid to the Bible, you would agree with me. But of what value is it if you do not use it?

I have seen the Bible change men. Some years ago one of my members told me that he was going to read the Bible through that year. As he began to read the Bible I saw him begin to grow in Christian grace. He was soon attending every service of the church, he was soon active in the work of the Lord and giving a tithe of his income. The Bible changed him and it will change you if you will only read it. If you are satisfied with the Christian life you are living, you don't need the Bible. If you want to be a better man, if you want to live more like Jesus, then you must read God's holy Word. Jesus loved the Word of God, do you?

III. Jesus Loved Prayer — So Should We

He was a man of prayer. He prayed from the cradle to the grave. I know that He must have prayed as a boy. He prayed at His baptism. He prayed during the forty days that He spent in the wilderness. He prayed as He performed His miracles and preached on the mountainside. He often prayed all night. He prayed at the grave of Lazarus. He prayed with a broken heart in the Garden of Gethsemane. He prayed upon the cross when He was dying for you and me. If Jesus, who was perfect, needed to pray, how much more do you and I who are so sinful need to pray? If Jesus, who had all power, needed to pray, how much more do we who are weaklings need to pray?

He loved prayer because of what prayer is. It is just talking to God. The psychologists try to make it hard, but the simple truth is that prayer is conversation and communion between a human being and his Heavenly Father. During the war both of our boys were in the Air Corps. Often our telephone would ring and the operator would tell us that she had a collect call for us. Always we would say, "Yes, we will accept the call, put him on." We had a big telephone bill every month, but what did we care? We had the joy of talking to our boys. Oh, don't you think God enjoys hearing from His children? He is never too busy. He is always listening. He rejoices to hear from us.

While God rejoices to hear from us, Satan fears prayer. "Satan trembles when he sees the weakest saint upon his knees." Why does Satan tremble? Because he knows that prayer will defeat him and break up all his plans. Here is a child of God who is being greatly tempted to sin. The devil cries out, "Aha, I have him. I will bring him down into sin." So the devil plans his work and works his plans. He paints a glowing picture of sin and brings fierce pressure upon the Christian. But the child of God cries out to heaven, "Oh Lord, deliver me. You know I am weak at this point. You know that Satan is after me. I need your help. Come and give me strength to overcome." And God sends down His angels of help and strength and the man is wondrously delivered. Satan then sneaks back to hell, defeated by prayer. The Psalmist said, "This poor man cried and the Lord heard him and saved him out of all of his troubles." Yes, Jesus loved prayer, do you?

IV. Jesus Loved Lost Souls — So Should We

That's why He left heaven's glory, that's why He turned His back upon God's House. That's why He came down to earth as the poorest of the poor, that's why He was willing to live a lonely life. That's why He endured blasphemies and falsehoods and evil names. That's why He sweat blood in Gethsemane and received the spittings and beatings of Pilate's court without murmur. That's why He carried the cross to Calvary. That's why He hung upon the nails. That's why He despised the shame and poured out His precious blood and gave up the ghost. He did it for you and me, because we were lost, lost, lost! He saw us going to hell and did everything to save us. "The Son of man came to seek and save that which was lost."

He came from the adoration of heaven to the agonies of earth to save the lost. He came from the blessings of heaven to the bruises of earth to save the lost. He came from the crown of heaven to the crucifixion of earth to save the lost. He came from the delights of heaven to the degradation of earth to save the lost. He came from the exaltation of heaven to the execution of earth to save the lost. He came from the fellowship of heaven to the floggings of earth to save the lost. He came from the glory of heaven to the ghastliness of earth to save the lost.

He loved lost souls. Do you? "Is it nothing to you, all you who pass by?" Don't you care whether men go to heaven or hell? You may never go to Japan or Africa, but through your gifts you may have a part in every soul saved over there. Then some day someone from there may meet you in heaven and say, "I am here because of you." Then you will say, "But I never saw you." But they will answer, "You never saw me, but you sent the Gospel to me and I was saved because you did it."

Some hunters were in the wild mountains of the Northwest. A flash flood broke upon them and one of them was drowned. They were going to bury the man, but not one of the hunters was a Christian and they could not give him a Christian burial. They were just going to cover him up and leave him there. Then the Indian guide said, "Is that the way that the white men bury their dead?" One of the hunters said, "No, but not one of us is a Christian and we don't know what to say." Then the Indian said, "I am a Christian, permit me to perform this service." The Indian stood by the grave and spoke of Christ with such beauty that some of the hunters were saved on the spot. One young man went home and said, "Mother, as that Indian spoke I gave my heart to the Lord." "Thank God," said the mother, "this is the way that the Lord has repaid me. Years ago I gave the first money to send missionaries to those Indians. Now you, my son, have been saved because of it." Maybe God is withholding some blessing from you because you do not love souls enough to give your money to send His Gospel to those who are lost. Yes, Jesus loved lost souls, do you?

V. Jesus Loved the Church — So Should We

Ephesians 5:25 — "Christ also loved the church and gave himself for it." Do we need to magnify that Scripture?

If Jesus founded the church and gave Himself for it and blessed it, we know that He loved it. God has given you a church home. You can go there to worship and to serve. You can have fellowship there with the finest people on earth. You can give your money through the church to a cause that will outshine the stars. The work of your church is a redemptive work. The end of all that we do and every penny that we spend is to lead someone to Christ. Where can you invest your time, talent and money where it will mean more?

There are various ways in which you can show your love to your church. First, by attending your church. "Forsake not the assembling of yourselves together." If a man loves Christ you can't keep him away from church. We can show our love for the church by praying for it. We ought to feel about the church like the Jews did about Jerusalem. They said, "If I forget thee, O Jerusalem, let my right hand forget her cunning. If I do not remember thee, let my tongue cleave to the roof of my mouth; if I prefer not Jerusalem above my chief joy."

We can show our love for the church by our service. Oh, for faithful servants of the Lord! Why do some Sunday school classes not have teachers? Why are some choir seats empty? Why are the deacons not all present? Why do we have empty pews on Sunday night? Why is the church not doing all that she could do? It is simply because our people are not the faithful Christians and church members that they ought to be.

Then we can show our love for Christ and His church by our giving. Every one can do that. Not all of us can preach or teach or sing, but every one can give his part. We are to bring our tithes and offerings unto the Lord. Every one can do that and this is one way in which we can do the will of the Lord perfectly. But you say that you can't afford to tithe. God declares that if we tithe He will pour out His blessings upon us. You are working against yourself when you do not tithe. God has laid down a rule for giving and it is best that we go by it. There are certain rules in medicine and the doctor finds it best to go by these rules. There are certain rules in law and the lawyer finds it best to go by these rules. There are certain rules in cooking and the cook finds it best to go by these rules. There are certain rules in sports and the athlete finds it best to go by these rules. And truly there are certain rules in Christianity and the Christian finds it best to go by these rules. God wrote the rules and He knows what is best for us.

A certain man joined the church of which I was pastor. He called me and told me that his income was $15,000 per year. He asked me what the average member gave. I suppose that he wanted to give the average. I told him that I could not give him the information he sought, but that I could give him what God said about giving. I proceeded to do that. The result was that the man did not give one penny. We must seek to go by God's rule and not by man's average. Another man came to me and said, "I must cancel my pledge. I am having a hard time." I told him that if he would tithe, God would take care of him. Some months later he came to me and said, "I am the happiest man in the world. What you said about tithing is true." Every man will find God's Word to be true.

I have seen what tithing can do for people. It is simply an act of obedience. Obedience to God always has a good effect upon His children. I have seen lives transformed by tithing. I have seen new Christians made out of old ones by tithing. On the other hand, I have watched those who knew that they should tithe but who refused to do it. I have seen them wither spiritually, lose their possessions and drift away from God. I never knew a man to grow in grace unless that man were a tither. However, in one way or another every man is a tither. He either gives the tithe to God and gets a joy out of it, or he may pay it out in some financial reverse and lose the joy. How much better it is to give as we should and to get the joy and the blessing.

One of the Christian's greatest sins is that of covetousness. Men want to hold on to things. They are afraid that if they give they will lose everything. But by God's plan we get more by giving than by holding. A certain Catholic Priest in New York City had been at the same church for twenty-five years. He said that in that time he had received many confessions. He said that all kinds of sin had been confessed except one, the sin of covetousness. Men hate to admit that they are holding something which does not belong to them.

I read recently of three young fellows who held up a filling station and took quite a sum of money. They were caught by the officers and brought to trial. They thought they were smart and they grinned all the way through the trial. However, when the stern judge gave them the full penalty of the law, their grins disappeared and they became pale and trembled. God, through Malachi, tells us that we are robbing Him when we do not tithe. You may think that a light thing now, but what will you say when you stand before the Judge, and He says, "I gave you all that you had in the world, but you withheld My part from Me"? God says that "the tithe is the Lord's." Then it isn't mine. My wife is mine, not yours. My car, my suit, my watch, all these are mine. They are not yours and you have no right to take them. Neither do you have a right to take that which belongs to God and use it for yourself. I challenge you to pay your tithe. There is only one way to do it. You must give the first tenth of your income. Then you will receive such a blessing that you will never want to go back to the old way.

Yes, Jesus loved the church and so should we. If He were to come to the platform some morning I believe that He would say to the pastor, "Stand aside for a while. I have something to say to these people." Then He would say to the congregation, "I want you to heed the call of this preacher's sermon. I want you to do all things that he has asked you to do. I want you to rededicate your life to Me and give Me the right-of-way in that life. If you are holding back anything from Me, I want you to surrender that thing. I gave My all for you, won't you give your best for Me? I want you to do what My preacher has asked you

to do this morning." What would you say to Jesus? Surely
if you loved Him you would say, "Lord, I do love Thee.
You can have my all. I will give my best for You."

An old man who had been a missionary for many years
lay on his death-bed in faraway India. A missionary who
had been there just two years came out to see him. The
young missionary said to the older missionary, "I have a
problem and I want you to help me with it. I have two
letters. One is from my home church in America asking me
to be their pastor. The other is from our Foreign Mission
Society asking me to serve as Mission Secretary. I don't
know what to do. Now you have been here a long time,
haven't you?" And the old man said, "Yes, I have been
here forty-seven years." "You don't have much to show
for it, do you?" And the old missionary said, "No." "Now,"
said the young missionary, "your wife and children are
gone. They died of tropical fever. They would have been
alive if you had not stayed in this country." "Yes," said the
old missionary, "you are right." "And you have quite a small
church, don't you?" "Yes, it's just a one-room building,
and we have fifty-three members." "Well," said the young
missionary, "you see what has happened to you. What
would you do if you were in my place? Would you stay in
the jungle or would you go back home to this great oppor-
tunity?"

The old man closed his eyes for a moment and the tears
ran down his cheeks. Then he opened his eyes and said,
"I am going to die soon and climb up to heaven. I will knock
on the Pearly Gates and the door-keeper will let me in.
After I register they will tell me to report to the Lord
Jesus. I will start down the golden street and a dark-skinned
Hindu girl will come tripping up to me. She will take
my hand in hers and say, 'Doctor, I have been waiting for
you. I am so glad to see you. You don't know me, but
you led me to Christ and baptized me. Would you mind
if I take you to see Jesus?' Then I will say, 'No, I will be
only too glad, my child.' We will then walk down the
glorious highway and soon we will approach the Throne of

Glory. Christ will step down from that Throne and come to meet me. I will be a bit frightened, but the girl will take hold of Jesus' hand and say, 'Lord Jesus, this man left his home and country and people to come to my land. He watched his wife and children suffer and die. He was the first one to tell me about You, now I want to be the first one to tell You about him.' " The old man stopped talking. The young man fell upon his knees by the bedside and said, "Doctor, I'll stick. I'll stay here."

Oh, my friends, you and I are not called upon to suffer like that, but we are called upon to be faithful and to support those who do go out in the Name of Christ. God help us to say, "Lord, I'll stick. I'll stick by Christ and the Church and the Great Commission. I'll stick by the Bible and prayer and the souls of lost men." So I ask you in closing, if in the Name of Jesus Christ and for the sake of His Church, won't you say, "He can count on me"?

2.

The Christian and His Sin
I John 1:1-10

The history of the world is the history of sin. In Genesis we see sin coming into the world. In Revelation we read of a life and land and time when there will be no sin. But all in between we see the sad story of sin. Everything that is good in this world was brought in by God. Everything that is bad was brought in by sin. The history of the individual is the same as the history of the world. Sin begins in us when we are born and continues with us until we get to heaven. We may have a great experience with the Lord, we may serve Him well over many years, but we will never get rid of our sins as long as we live.

I speak now about a Christian and his sin. Don't ever get the idea that you can live in sinless perfection after you are saved. You are going to be tempted and because you are human you are going to sin. Paul had a tremendous conversion experience, but after that he often cried out about his sin. John was closer to Jesus than any of the disciples, but he said that any man who said that he had not sinned was a liar. So let us think about the Christian and his sin, as follows:

I. THE CHRISTIAN'S SIN AS TO THE PAST
II. THE CHRISTIAN'S SIN AS TO THE PRESENT
III. THE CHRISTIAN'S SIN AS TO THE FUTURE

I. THE CHRISTIAN'S SIN AS TO THE PAST

1. *He was born in sin.* The Bible rings out with the truth that we have sin in us when we come into the world. But if we didn't have a Bible we would know that this is true.

24

Just watch a tiny baby. If he doesn't get his way he screams out and his face turns red and he lets us know that he has something in him which was there when he was born. That something is sin. A teacher asked a Sunday school class the question, "Do we have anything that we didn't get from God?" A little girl wisely answered, "Yes, we have our sins." That is certainly true. Our sins arise out of our Adamic nature. We are born with sin in us. Now just let a little child have his own way, never correct him, never discipline him, never deny him anything, and what will happen? That sin with which he was born will assert itself and he will try to run rough-shod over the world. This will be further proof that the sin was there when he was born.

2. *Then he continues in sin.* Man is not only born in sin, he continues in that sin. "All have sinned and come short of the glory of God." The trouble with so many of us today is that we look upon sin in a comparative manner. We look at someone who is really deep down in sin and we say, "I am certainly not as bad as that fellow." So we excuse our own sin because it is not as black as the other fellow's sin.

Imagine a man on trial for stealing $1,000. He says to the presiding officer, "Judge, you know that I stole this money, but you can't blame me. There are many others worse than I am. I read of one fellow who stole $10,000." But what the other fellow does will not lessen your guilt. Your sin is your own. It belongs to no one else. Though all men are worse sinners than you, this doesn't cancel out the fact of your sin.

Now what do we mean when we say that a person "continues in sin"? What is sin? It is anything that God does not approve of. It may be the sin of commission, doing something which God strictly forbids. It could be dishonesty, drinking, adultery, lying or cheating. It could be one of a thousand things. It may be the sin of omission. "To him that knoweth to do good and doeth it not, it is sin." You know it is a good thing for a Christian to get into a church, to be faithful, to pay his tithe and to serve the

Lord. If you don't do these things you are committing a sin just as surely as if you had robbed a bank.

It may be the sin of disobedience. God has commanded you to be baptized, He may have called upon you to serve Him in some certain way. Yet you continue to say, "No" to God. That is a sin. Your sin may be the wrong attitude of heart. It may be envy, jealousy, malice or hatred. No one has to tell you when you have sinned, you are intelligent. You know when you have sinned.

3. *He was lost in his sin.* Not only was the Christian born in sin, not only did he continue in sin, but he was lost in that sin. The Bible said that he was condemned. The Bible said that he would not see God. The Bible said that he was going to hell.

4. *Then he was convicted for sin.* There came a glorious day when the man in his sin saw the folly of that sin. He saw that he was lost. God was convicting him through His Holy Spirit. What does conviction mean? Jesus illustrates. He tells of the publican who came to church. He saw good people all around him but he realized that he was not good. He saw men worshiping God, but he realized that sin stood between him and God. He saw himself as God saw him and cried out, "God be merciful to me a sinner." He was really convicted for sin. When you joined the church was there any conviction for sin connected with it? Did you see yourself as a lost sinner? Did you feel that you deserved hell and that you were not worthy of God's grace? That was conviction.

5. *Then he saw a Saviour dying for him.* On an old rugged cross he saw a Man dying. The Holy Spirit told him that this Man was dying for him, to save him from his sin. Then his heart broke and his eyes filled with tears. "Can it be really true?" he asked. "Did God love me that much? Did Christ really die for me?" And the answer came from heaven, "Yes, I loved you that much. I gave My Only Begotten Son for your redemption." Then the Man on the cross spoke and said, "Come unto Me, for him that cometh to Me, I will in no wise cast out." And the sinner said,

"I am coming. I need Christ. Here, Lord, I give myself to Thee, 'tis all that I can do."

And that very moment his sins were forgiven. Joy filled his heart. Gratitude surged through his soul. He said, "I am going to love Jesus and serve Him all the days of my life." You remember that when Moses died God buried him. The Bible tells us that no one knows where Moses is buried. God not only buried Moses, but He also buried the grave and the graveyard. That's what God does with our sins. He buries them, He forgives and forgets. If a Christian met Him today and asked, "Lord, where did you bury my sins?", I believe that the Lord would say, "I don't know."

> When God forgives, He forgets,
> When God forgives, He forgets,
> No longer He remembers our sins,
> When God forgives, He forgets.

The other day I read an article by a man who is ninety years of age. He said, "I did three things as a boy and a young man which I have been ashamed of all these years. They still haunt me and hurt me." I wanted to say to him, "Man, have you never heard of God's forgiveness and forgetfulness?"

So there we see the Christian's sins as to the past. He was born in sin, he continued in sin, he was convicted for sin, but he came to the Saviour and now all of his sins have been forgiven.

II. THE CHRISTIAN'S SIN AS TO THE PRESENT

1. *First, he will be often tempted.* As long as you are following sin, the devil is not going to bother you. He knows that he has you already. But the minute you come to Christ, Satan gets busy. He tries to tempt you and draw you away from Christ. He would rather do that than anything in the world. Man is born with a sinful nature. The Bible calls it "the carnal nature." When we are converted, we still have that carnal nature, but God gives us a new nature. Then there begins a continual warfare between the two natures. One nature pulls up and the other nature down.

One nature pulls toward good and the other toward evil.
You will lose the battle if you don't get close to God and
seek His help.

2. *Then the Christian sometimes falls before temptation.*
No Christian is able to stand against all the wiles of the
devil. There will come a time when he falls before temptation, for there has never been a perfect man except Christ.
But when a real Christian sins, he becomes miserable. His
sin breaks his fellowship with God. When a real Christian feels that there is something between him and God
he cannot be happy. Do you think that Peter was happy
after he denied Christ? No, he was miserable until he was
back in the arms of Jesus.

A Christian was thrown into jail by order of the Roman
Emperor. The Emperor called in his counselor and said,
"What shall we do with him? Shall we confiscate his goods?"
And the counselor said, "That will not harm him, for he
says that he possesses unsearchable riches in Christ." "Shall
we put him in prison?" asked the Emperor. "That will
not hurt him, for he says that he has a Friend who will
never leave him nor forsake him." Then the Emperor
asked, "Shall we cut off his head?" The counselor answered,
"He would like that, he says that to die is gain, that it
is far better to depart and be with Christ." "What then,"
asked the Emperor, "do you advise as the worst punishment
that we can give him?" The counselor answered, "There is
only one thing that can give him great pain. We must get
him to sin." Ah, sin ought to be the thing that hurts us
most. When a Christian sins he ought to be miserable. He
is out of his element. His fellowship with Christ is broken.

When Eudocia threatened to banish Chrysostom, the
great man said, "Go and tell Eudocia that the only thing
I fear is sin." Again he said, "The only calamity is sin,
for everything else let God be praised." That's the way
we ought to feel about sin.

Why is it that so many of our people who profess to be
Christians live for the world and do nothing for God? It is

because they let sin break their fellowship with God. They don't feel their need of Him any more.

3. *But God provides a way to forgiveness when a Christian sins.* Here it is, "If we confess our sins, He is faithful and just to forgive us our sins, and to cleanse us from all unrighteousness." Does this simply mean that we are to notify God of what we have done? No, it includes telling God about it, it includes forsaking that sin and asking God to forgive it. Now examine yourself today. Think about your sin. Let your memory bring it back and hold it up before your gaze. Look at it. It isn't pretty, is it? As you sit in God's house, don't you see how ugly it is? Go before the Lord and say, "Dear God, here is my sin. I am through with it. Forgive me and cleanse me and give me a new start."

And He will. I know He will. David's sin was greater than yours, yet God forgave him and restored happiness to him. Peter's sin was great, but the Lord forgave him and made him a great servant of the Saviour. And what He has done for others, He will do for you.

4. *But often the consequences of sin remain.* A man kills another. In prison he hears the Gospel and is saved. But this doesn't bring the other man back. It doesn't cut down the guilty man's sentence. The Christian's sins are punished in this world. The sinner's punishment is reserved for hell. David was a man after God's own heart. God plucked him out of a shepherd's field and made him a great king. He did mighty things for God. He wrote wonderful Psalms about God. But one day David sinned. He broke at least four of the Ten Commandments. He put the god of lust before the God of heaven. He coveted another man's wife. He committed adultery. He indirectly killed the woman's husband.

The time came when God forgave David, but that forgiveness didn't nullify the consequences of his sin. From that day the sword never departed from his house. He never had another completely happy day. Surely often in the silence of his room he cried out, "Oh, God, what a fool

I was! I wish I hadn't sinned as I did. You have been so good to me, I am sorry that I sinned against Thee." David is up in heaven now and I am sure that all of this has been forgotten, but he paid an awful price for his sin. So will you, my friend. So I call on you to leave your sins. Cry out to God to forgive you and cleanse you and give you a new start. What about it, backslider? What about it, sinful Christian?

III. The Christian's Sin As to the Future

One day the Christian is going to soar up to be with the Lord. It won't be long now. And when he goes, all of his sin will be left behind. He will be changed into the likeness of Christ and sin will nevermore have dominion over him.

There will be no penalty for sin in heaven. That penalty was paid on Calvary's Cross. In heaven there will be no punishment for the evil deeds of this world. There will be no presence of sin in heaven. Down here we come in contact with sin on every side, tempting us and dragging us down. But there will be nothing defiling in heaven. There will be no remembrance of sin in heaven. Down here our sins have been forgiven, but we can't help but think of them with sorrow once in a while. Up there our sins will be buried in the sea of forgetfulness.

In 1951 some doctors in an Ohio penitentiary wanted to make an experiment. They believed that an operation on a man's brain would change him and rid him of criminal tendencies. A prisoner in that prison submitted to the operation. But the operation was a failure. The man was released from prison, but soon he was back in again for forgery. In order for a man to be changed, he must have a changed heart. Only Christ can give that. While this sermon is directed primarily to Christians, I plead also with you who have not been born again to come to Christ. Let Him give you a new heart, a new life, a new nature, a new hope. He makes all things new when you come to Him.

Down in Australia a boy and his father quarreled and in the heat of the moment the father told the boy to get his clothes and leave home. The boy gathered a few things together and went out the door never to return. In the years that followed, the family often wondered what had become of the boy. They hoped that one day he would come back, but he never did. One night a preacher was visiting in the home and the mother suggested that he might be interested in a ritual which they performed every night. She then stepped out of the front door and put the door key under the mat. She explained to the preacher that when the boy was living at home, they always left the key under the mat so that he could get into the house if he came in late. "Now," she told the preacher, "if he should come back some night wondering whether or not we wanted him back, all that he would have to do would be to look under the door mat and see the key and know that he was welcome."

Listen, my friend, God doesn't just leave the key outside. He leaves the door of mercy and forgiveness wide open. He is waiting to receive you and give you His best. Why don't you walk in that door?

3.

The Christian and His Sorrows
Psalm 30

Several years ago five wonderful missionaries went with their families to the interior of Ecuador. A tribe of Indians was living there in the jungle. They had never heard the Gospel. They had never been touched by civilization. These five young men felt that God wanted them to take Christ to these Indians. They set up their headquarters and flew in their private plane over the territory each day. They saw these Indians, dropped presents to them, and did everything they could to show that they were friendly. The time came when they felt it was safe to land in a cleared space on the banks of a river. So they flew over and landed, all the time keeping in touch with their wives at headquarters by means of radio. Suddenly the wives who were listening heard one of the men say, "Here comes another group of Indians that we haven't seen before." Then the radio went dead. An agonizing silence ensued. These women didn't know what had happened to their husbands. All night long they waited, but received no word from them. Another plane flew over the area the next morning and found the five missionaries dead on the banks of the river. The hearts of the wives and children were broken, but they decided to stay on in Ecuador and take the Gospel to the men who had killed their husbands. Now they are doing a great work there. They have been received by these Indians and they are winning some of them to Christ. This is one of the greatest missionary stories of modern times.

Can you imagine the sorrow of these women? They

kissed their husbands good-by, saw them fly away with
high hopes, and then came the heart-breaking news that
they were dead. You and I have never had a sorrow that
deep. But all of us have had sorrows of some kind. We
know what it is to shed tears and to have a broken heart.
If you young people have not had any sorrow in your lives
up to this time, let me tell you that in due time they will
come. Sorrow is one traveler which every one of us meets
on the road of life.

Does a Christian have sorrow? Does one who loves
Christ shed tears? Does one who is living for God ever
have a broken heart? Yes, a thousand times, yes. We are
living in a world of sin and sin brings sorrow. Sorrow is the
common lot of us all. I want to discuss this with you from
three aspects:

I. THE PREVALENCE OF SORROW
II. THE PURPOSE OF SORROW
III. THE PRESENCE OF GOD IN SORROW

I. THE PREVALENCE OF SORROW

Someone has said, "God had one Son without sin, but no
son without sorrow." Yes, Jesus had His sorrows. He was
indeed "a man of sorrows and acquainted with grief." No
man ever had the sorrow which came to Jesus. The Bible men
of old had their sorrow. David said, "Man is born to trouble
as the sparks fly upward." The greatest men of history had
their sorrow. When you read their biographies you see that
these were the things which made them great. The people
whom you know have their sorrows. You look at someone
and say, "He has no trouble. He has money, he has good
health, he has security, he has a nice family. He has nothing
to worry about." But deep down underneath, that man may
bear secret burdens which you know nothing about. And
you and I have our sorrows. Some of them can be seen by
the whole world. Some are hidden to all but the eye of God.

The causes of sorrow are varied. Some sorrows come as
a consequence of our departing from God. Some sorrows
come from poverty, some come from wealth. Some sorrows

come from domestic trouble, and some come from the loss of loved ones. A preacher friend of mine died three years ago. His wife is a fine Christian woman, but she just can't seem to adjust herself to his death. She carries a heavy heart of sorrow. Some sorrow comes from our deliberate sin. Some sorrows come from man's inhumanity to man. Some come from the unworthy lives of some member of the family.

Our evening paper in El Paso has a little column on the front page which tells us how many consecutive days of sunshine we have had. Recently I read that in the last 1,055 days there had been only six days without sunshine. However, life is different. We don't have many cloudless days. Sorrow is present on every side and no one is exempt.

II. The Purpose of Sorrow

Some people are naturally pessimistic. They never see good in anything. Certainly they cannot see any benefit in sorrow. A fable tells about two frogs that fell into a large can of milk. One of them was named Pessimist. He said, "What's the use of going on kicking? I will drown sooner or later, so I might as well give up now." He sank to the bottom of the can and was immediately drowned. The other frog was named Optimist. He kept on kicking. The next morning when the can was opened, there he was sitting on a pad of butter. He had made the right use of his adversity.

Now when sorrow comes to men they ask the age-old question, "Why?" They say, "Why does a Christian have to suffer like this?" Christians who are living for God ask this question, and Christians who are not faithful ask the same question. We can't find a full answer in this life, but maybe we can find a partial answer. Let us try.

1. *Sorrow comes to teach us that God's grace is sufficient for every need.* Paul tells us that he had a thorn in the flesh. We don't know what it was, but it was a thing that hurt him and burdened him. So he went to the Lord three times and asked Him to remove the thorn, and God said, "No, Paul, I am not going to remove the thorn, but

just remember that My grace is sufficient for thee." And
Paul said that he would glory in his infirmities, that he
might have this extra grace. But Paul never would have
known the fullness of God's grace unless he had needed it.
So you and I will never know all that God can mean to us
until trouble comes. The food on your table may be the
finest in the world, but if you are not hungry, if you don't
eat the food, you will never know how good it is. And you
and I will never know how good God's grace is until something comes which makes us partake of it. In the light
you feel that you can walk alone, but in the darkness you
feel that you need to reach out and touch His hand and
it is then that a great peace floods your soul.

Spurgeon seemingly came to a time of deep depression.
Then he read the text, "My grace is sufficient for thee." This
truth came with such force that his gloom was lifted and
he began to laugh. In telling about it he said, "Imagine a
tiny fish fearing that he could drink the river dry and the
river saying to him, 'Poor little fish, my water is sufficient
for thee.' Then imagine a little mouse in a great granary,
fearing that he might die of famine, and the granary saying, 'Cheer up, little mouse, my grain is sufficient for thee.'
Then imagine a man on the top of a high mountain, fearing lest he breathe up all the air in the universe, and the
earth saying to him, 'Breathe away, little man, my air is
sufficient for thee.'" Then the great preacher said, "Imagine
a man thinking that he will go down forever because
maybe God's grace will fail him. Oh, if your needs were a
million times greater God would supply them all." Yes,
in sorrow we learn the greatness of God's grace.

2. *Then sorrow brings us closer to God.* Often a Christian gets far away from God. He quits going to church,
he seems to forget about God. Then God sends a sorrow
to bring him back and to make him feel his desperate need
of the Lord. When I was a boy we had a dog, but when
we went out walking together he would run far ahead and it
was hard to keep him close at hand. But one thing he
liked to do. I would throw a stick and he would run and

get it and bring it back and lay it at my feet. So we often go far away from God and He sends us a sorrow that we cannot handle. We find that we must bring it to God's feet. Isn't it better to have a sorrow and to live close to God, than to be without sorrow and be far away from God?

I have had many people say to me when sorrow came, "Preacher, I know I have not been living rightly. I am coming back to church and I am going to live closer to God." It takes a sorrow to bring them. A Sunday school teacher read the Scripture verse, "My yoke is easy," to a class of girls. She asked the girls to describe a yoke. One of them said that it was something that you put on the neck of animals. Then the teacher asked, "What is the meaning of God's yoke?" And the girl answered, "It is God putting His arms around our neck." That is one purpose of sorrow. It is a loving God putting His arms around our necks and drawing us closer to Him.

3. *Then sorrow comes to develop Christian character.* Men are not developed by pleasures but by sorrow. The Christian who has never known sorrow is not as fully developed as the one who has walked through the dark valley. The best pictures in the photographer's shop are developed in the darkest room. And it is in the dark rooms of life that we are developed into more Christ-like Christians.

The women in a certain Sunday school class read the Scripture in Malachi 3:3, "He shall sit as a refiner and purifier of silver." One of the ladies decided to go to a silversmith to see what this verse meant. She found him sitting before a crucible, gazing intently into the boiling pot. She asked him, "Do you have to sit there all the time while the work of refining is going on?" And he answered, "Yes, I must sit here with my eye on the crucible. If it gets too hot, the silver will be injured." Then she saw the meaning of the text. God puts us in the furnace of affliction, but He watches to see that it never gets hot enough to injure us. These things hurt us but they do not injure us. Then the silversmith said one more thing, "I know that the process of purifying is completed when I see my own image reflected in the silver." And God knows when we have been purified. It is when His image is reflected in us.

4. *Sorrow comes to enable us to help others.* A Virginia mother lost her only child. However, instead of shutting herself up with her grief, she turned that grief into something useful. She took a job as superintendent of the Junior Department of her church. Through the years she influenced scores of boys and girls who now hold leadership positions around the world. Thousands of people today who are sitting in self-created misery would soon lose it if they began to care for others. When you dig another man out of trouble, you can bury your own troubles in that same hole. The sorrows of life ought to make us more responsive to the needs of others.

A woman in Oklahoma lost one of her sons in an automobile accident. He had been a victorious Christian, but there was another son who was not a Christian. This mother said to the preacher who was going to conduct the funeral, "I want you to preach for the soul of my unsaved son. I am praying for him to come to Christ." God answered her prayer, for the son was saved and became a radiant Christian.

We conjugate verbs by saying, "I am, you are, he is." You remember the words in Latin, *"Amo, Amas, Amat,"* meaning "I love, you love, he loves." But the Hebrew of the Old Testament is different. The conjugation there is as follows, "He is, you are, I am." You look up to God and say, "He is." You look out to others and say, "You are." You look last at yourself and say, "I am." When we have sorrow we are often taught that self is not to be put first, but God and others. Yes, sorrow often fits us to be a blessing to someone else.

III. THE PRESENCE OF GOD IN SORROW

God has promised never to forsake us. This means that He will be just as close to us in the time of sorrow as in the time of joy, if not even closer. A child goes from El Paso out to the West Coast and sees the great Pacific Ocean.

He comes back and says, "I have seen the ocean." It is true that he has seen a few miles of the ocean, but he saw nothing of the wide expanse which reaches all the way to Asia. So a man can say, "I know God. I have come to know him through faith in Jesus Christ." That is true, but he doesn't know God in all of His love and sweetness and grace until he knows Him in sorrow.

Spurgeon visited a farmer friend and saw a weathervane on his barn, with the words, "God Is Love," painted under the weathervane. Mr. Spurgeon asked, "Do you mean to say that God's love is as changeable as the wind?" "Oh, no," said the farmer, "I am saying that God is love whichever way the wind blows."

Nothing can separate us from the love of God. Romans 8:35-39, "Who shall separate us from the love of Christ? Shall tribulation, or distress, or persecution, or famine, or nakedness, or peril, or sword? As it is written, for thy sake we are killed all the day long; we are accounted as sheep for the slaughter. Nay, in all these things we are more than conquerors through Him that loved us. For I am persuaded, that neither death, nor life, nor angels, nor principalities, nor powers, nor things present, nor things to come, nor height, nor depth, nor any other creature, shall be able to separate us from the love of God, which is in Christ Jesus our Lord."

Trials cannot separate us, for it was said of Joseph that God was with him in his trials. Sorrows cannot separate us, for He assures us that He will be with us when we pass through the deep waters. Danger cannot separate us, for He was with the three Hebrew children in the fiery furnace. But while we are saved and never separated from God, our sin, our worldliness, our backsliding, and our neglect of spiritual things can cut us off from communion with God and peace of heart.

Are you drinking the cup of sorrow? Then turn it around and read the other side. You will find it encircled with God's love. For we read that, "All things work together for good to them that love God. . . . As thy days shall demand, so shall thy strength ever be. . . . As one whom his mother comforteth, so will I comfort you. . . . My grace is sufficient for you."

Yes, on one side of the scales of life we find sorrows and troubles, but on the other side we find the love and comfort of the Heavenly Father, far outweighing anything that can ever touch us. "I reckon that the sufferings of the present time are not to be compared to the glory which shall be revealed in us. . . . Our light afflictions which are but for a moment, worketh for us a far more exceeding and eternal weight of glory."

A London girl went down into sin, breaking her mother's heart. Her mother came to her pastor and pled for his help. He said to her, "Go home and bring me every picture of yourself that you have." The next day the woman brought several pictures to the pastor, and on the bottom of each picture he wrote in red ink the letters, "Come home." He then went out and put these pictures in several places of sin in the city. One night the girl, with a sinful companion, came into one of these places and suddenly saw before her the picture of her mother. The tears welled up in her eyes and when she brushed the tears away, she saw those precious words, "Come home." Without a word to her companion in sin, she left that place, went across the city and back to the old home. She found the door unlocked and when she opened it her mother rushed forward and gathered her in her arms, saying, "My darling, I knew that you would come home some night and the door has always been left unlocked."

That's what God is saying to you today. To the lost He says, "Come home and be saved." To the Christian He says, "Come home from all of your sins and shortcomings and griefs, and I will forgive you and bless you and comfort you."

4.

The Christian and His Future Prospects
John 14:1-6

The child of God has a glorious past. He remembers that Christ loved him enough to die on a cross for him, he remembers how Christ has saved him and blessed him along life's pathway. He also has a joyous present. The Lord blesses him at every turn, he has the high privilege of walking and talking daily with the King. But as wonderful as the past has been and as fine as the present time is, the Christian's future prospects are a million times more blessed and more glorious than anything he has ever experienced.

The orthodox Jews, in building their houses, always left some part unfinished. This was to remind them that they were just pilgrims here, that this life was an unfinished thing and they were traveling toward eternity. So, that which you and I enjoy today in Christ is but a part of the whole. All the joys of a glorious future are awaiting us.

Some people have no future prospects. They walk in the darkness of sin and unbelief. One day they will come to the end of the way. They will be forced to say what one unbeliever said, "I am taking a fearful leap into the darkness." Nothing good awaits them out there in the future. Not so with the Christian. His future prospects are as bright as the shining sun and as sure as God Himself.

The Christian's future is bright as to old age. The devil has no happy old people, but God's old people are His special care. The Christian's future is bright as to death. He can say, "Yea, though I walk through the valley of the shadow of death, I will fear no evil." The Christian's future is bright as to the life to come. He knows that he has a home in heaven awaiting him. I would like to discuss with you three things in this message:

I. The Light at Eventide
II. The Lord at the End of the Way
III. The Life of Eternal Glory

I. The Light at Eventide

This is the promise of God — that those who are His shall have light when the shadows lengthen. Nothing is more pitiful than an old person who has no hope, one who looks back over his life and can see no time when he and Christ met each other in the glorious experience of the new birth. And nothing is more wonderful to see than an old person coming to the end of the way filled with happy memories of great experiences and good times with Christ.

Now old age is inevitable if we keep on living. Just as in nature we have spring, summer, autumn and winter, so in human life we have infancy, childhood, youth, middle age and old age. But these days should bring no sorrow. This should be a time to thank God for all that is past and a time for looking forward to future joys.

> They call it going down the hill when we are growing old;
> And speak with mournful accents when our years are nearly told;
> They sigh when talking of the past — the days that used to be —
> As if the future were not bright with immortality.
> But oh! it is not going down, 'tis climbing higher — higher,
> Until we almost see the mansions that our souls desire.
> For if the natural eye grows dim, it is but dim to earth,
> While the eye of faith grows keener, to perceive the Saviour's worth.
> Those by-gone days, tho' days of joy, we wish not back again;
> Were there not also many days of sorrow and of pain?
> But in the days awaiting us, the days beyond the tomb

Sorrow shall find no place, but joys unmarred forever bloom.
For tho' in truth the outward man must perish and decay
The inner man shall be renewed by grace from day to day;
They who are planted by the Lord, unshaken in their root,
E'en in old age shall flourish and still bring forth rich fruit.
It is not years that make men old, the spirit may be young,
Though for the threescore years and ten the wheels of life
    have run;
God has Himself recorded, in His blessed Word of truth
That they who wait upon the Lord, these shall renew their
    youth.
And when the eyes, now dim, shall open to behold the King,
And ears, now dull with age, shall hear the harps of heaven
    ring,
And on the head, now hoary, shall be placed the crown of
    gold,
Then shall be known the lasting joy of never growing old.

Now let us look at some of the compensations of old age.
First there are many sweet memories. As we look back
over life we seem to forget all the hardships and to remember only the sweet and beautiful things. My wife and I
sometimes think of the time when we came west to the
seminary. We had one little boy four years of age and one
five months old. We had lots of baggage and we couldn't
afford to hire a red-cap to carry it. We got off the train at
the station in Fort Worth and walked down the street
toward the carline. We were all wrinkled and dirty from
several days on the train. I held the baby in my arms. He had
lost one of his little bootees. My wife led the other boy and
we went down to a "greasy spoon" restaurant and ate some
greasy food. We didn't have an automobile and we couldn't
afford a taxi, so we boarded a street car, baggage and all,
and rode out to the seminary. We had to stay in the dormi-
tory for a week before we could move into our little three-
room house. We were afraid to leave the baby on the bed
for fear the big Texas roaches would devour him. My wife
cried for a week because I had brought her a thousand miles
from home. We thought we were having a pretty rough
time then, but now we can laugh about it. This is one of the
compensations of growing old.

Another compensation is that of having happy anticipations. The young people don't think much about heaven because they haven't lost any loved ones. But the older person has lost many friends and loved ones, and he is often in poor health himself. So he looks forward with happy anticipation to the time when he will greet his loved ones again and when he will enjoy perfect health. Yes, there are many compensations in old age for the Christian. He looks back over his life with happy memories and he looks forward with joy and anticipation to the brighter life to come. But the old person without Christ has none of these things. Yes, this is a wonderful promise, that God would give us light at eventide.

II. The Lord at the End of the Way

You and I are not going to live forever. One of two things is going to happen. First, death may come. While I was preparing this chapter my phone rang. A friend was calling me to tell me that a preacher friend of mine had gone to a certain meeting, had suffered a heart attack, and had died a few hours later in the hospital. Yet he was not an old man. Second, Christ may come in the air and take us up to be with Him without dying. That will be a glorious experience. But whether we go by the way of death or whether we soar up to meet Him in the air, the Christian will be forever with the Lord.

Some of our loved ones have already gone. We see an empty bird's nest in a tree in the dead of winter. It looks sad and desolate and forsaken. But we know that the birds have gone to the Southland beyond the reach of the stormy winds. We know that they are singing just as sweetly there as they did here. There is an empty nest in many a home, but we know that the loved ones have gone on to a better land and are living there more wondrously than they did here.

A certain nobleman had a spacious garden which he left to the care of a faithful servant. In due time the garden brought forth an abundance of beautiful flowers. The caretaker was justly proud of them. Then one morning he came to the garden to find the choicest blossoms gone. In anger he rushed to the servants' quarters to learn who had picked his most beautiful flowers. He was told that the master had been to the garden early and had plucked the flowers for his table. His anger ceased and joy filled his heart. He was glad that his master had taken the flowers. Have you lost a loved one who was very dear to your heart? Your heart is broken, you miss them very much. Remember, my beloved, the Master has taken them. They are all right. They are in the Father's house of many mansions right now.

We need to remember that this world is simply our temporary dwelling place. So many people work hard for the things of this earth. They pile up material wealth and act as if they were going to live here forever. In one of his essays Addison tells of a traveler who went one night into a king's palace. Thinking it was an inn, he lay down on the soft carpet and went to sleep. The guard found him there and brought him before the king. The king asked, "How could you be so stupid as to think that this palace was an inn?" And the man said, "Let me ask you a question. Who lived here in this house when it was built?" "My ancestors," answered the king. "And who lived here before you?" asked the man. "My father." Then the man asked, "Who will live here after you?" And the king answered, "My son, the prince." "Ah sir," said the man, "a house that changes inhabitants so often is not a palace, it is an inn." How true that is. The Bible tells us to make the best of life, yet it reminds us always that this world is not our home. We are just passing through on the way to eternity.

But the Christian is to have no fear of death. A beautiful young woman lay dying and her father was broken with grief. "Father," she said, "you should not grieve so. If I were going to marry some young man that you approved of and who could give me all that my heart desired, but who was going to move to another city, you would not grieve.

Now I am going to be promoted to a position with Christ far above all that this world can offer. You should not grieve about that."

So the Christian should have no fear of death. It simply means a translation to a better life and a higher position than he can ever have in this world. We hear much talk about Russia dropping bombs on America and destroying us all. We are being urged to build bomb shelters. But why should the Christian worry? Let the bombs drop. This will only serve to send us to be with Christ, which is far better.

All the promises of God light up a death bed for the Christian. A young preacher was called on to visit a dying saint, eighty-seven years of age, who was a devout Christion. The preacher asked God to give him a message for the time. When he entered the room the old man said to him, "Pastor, I am dying. For years I have been feasting upon the promises of God, but this morning I can't remember a single one of them." God gave the words to the young preacher and he said, "Dear friend, do you think that God has forgotten any of His promises?" The old man answered, "Praise God, He will remember, won't He?" And you and I know that He will remember His promises and be with us at the end of the way.

My soul amid this stormy world is like some fluttering dove,
And fain would be as swift of wing to fly to Him above;
The cords that bound my heart to earth were broken by His
    Hand,
Before His throne I found myself a stranger in the land.
That visage marred, those sorrows deep, the vinegar, the
    gall —
These were the golden chains of love His captive to enthrall.
My heart is with Him on the throne, and ill can brook delay,
Each moment listening for the Voice: "Rise up, and come
    away!"
With hope deferred, oft sick and faint: "Why tarries He?"
    I cry:
"May not an exile, Lord, desire his own sweet land to see?
May not a captive seek release — a prisoner, to be free?"

A child, when far away, may long for home and kindred dear;
And she that waits her absent lord may sigh till he appear.
I would my Lord and Saviour know, that which no measure
knows —
Would search the mystery of Thy love, the depths of all
thy woes.
I fain would strike my golden harp before the Father's throne,
There cast my crown of righteousness and sing what grace
has done!
Ah, leave me not in this dark world a stranger still to roam;
Come, Lord, and take me to Thyself! Come, Jesus — quickly
come.

III. The Life of Eternal Glory

Old age may come and then death or the coming of
Christ, and then eternal glory. This is one reason I am glad
I am not a Catholic. A Catholic believes that when he dies,
he must go to purgatory and burn and suffer. No one wants
to look forward to a thing like that. No, you and I know
that Christ has done all the suffering necessary. So when a
Christian dies, his spirit goes to be with the Lord. This
is the plain teaching of the Word of God.

In that day our trials will all be over. We will never be
tempted again. We will never sin again. We will never
weep again. We will never be in trouble again. *Revelation* 21:4 says, "And God shall wipe away all tears from their
eyes; and there shall be no more death, neither sorrow, nor
crying, neither shall there be any more pain: for the former
things are passed away."

All the weariness and misunderstandings and bereavements will be over. Our polluted garments will be exchanged for robes of white. Every groan will be turned
into a hallelujah. Every tear will be changed into smiles
and laughter. A certain preacher contended all of his life for
the atonement of Christ against the hyper-critics of his day.
When he came to the end of the way, a friend commended
him for his loyal stand. He replied, "I am going now to a
place where the atonement is no longer a subject of controversy, but heaven's theme song." Yes, up there all of us

will sing the song of the One who died to bring us safely home.

Now who is going to be in heaven? God the Father, God the Son, and God the Holy Spirit will be there. We don't know whether we will see the Trinity as three distinct persons or as one. We must wait until we get there to find out. But the Christian dead will be there and our names will be there. Our citizenship is there, our reward is there, our inheritance is there, our treasure is there.

Shall we know each other in heaven? The Bible has no direct reference to heavenly recognition, but strongly infers that we will know each other there. When David lost his baby he said, "I shall go to him, but he shall not return to me." He surely meant that he expected to recognize his child in heaven. Jesus said that we would sit down with Abraham and Isaac and Jacob in the Kingdom of heaven. This certainly meant that the personal identity of these men would remain. Moses and Elijah died centuries before Christ was born, yet their personalities remained and they were recognized on the Mount of Transfiguration. Our transfer from earth to heaven does not destroy our personal identity. In every heart there is a desire to see and know their loved ones again. That desire surely is not opposed to the will of God.

We have learned in this sermon that in our old age God will be with us to comfort and sustain. We have learned that in death He will be there to hold our hands as we go through the dark valley. We have learned that in the life to come we will be there with Him to enjoy the bliss and the glory of heaven forever. The Christian has a bright prospect. He ought to appreciate it and spend his life serving the One who made it possible. The lost man has no such bright prospect, but he ought to come to the Christ who stands ready to give it to him.

Jesus spoke of Christians as "My sheep." He said on one occasion that His sheep would never perish. I have often heard a young husband proudly introduce his bride by saying, "This is my wife." Then years later I have visited the couple and taking me to the little bed, they have pointed to a sleeping child and said, "This is our baby." But let me tell you something more wonderful. One day because of Christ, you and I will go up the long steep road that leads to Glory. Then Jesus will put His arm around us and present us to the Father. He will say, "This is My child. Down in the world he trusted Me and confessed Me before men." And the Great Father will say, "Give him the best that we have in heaven. Nothing is too good for a child of God." And then the toils of the road will seem nothing. Just to see His blessed face and hear His sweet voice will be worth it all. Will this be your experience? Do you have this bright prospect for the future?

5.

Christ's Challenge to Christians
Matthew 16:21-27

Jesus Christ never calls men to the little things of life. He was big Himself, He came into the world to do big things, He calls us to do big things. Today we often want to follow the man who points out an easy way. But Jesus points out the hard way and challenges us to follow Him. No other course is worthy of a true Christian. It is an attractive thing to follow Christ, but it is no bed of roses. His call is to the highest and the hardest.

Now life is full of challenges. The business man is challenged to work hard and gain wealth. The professional man is challenged to serve well and make a name for himself. The student is challenged to get an education. And anyone who has the right stuff in him can get a good education today. Some people are challenged to gain notoriety. Years ago two men by the names of Loeb and Leopold killed a boy simply to gain notice. The woman who works hard to get her name and picture on the society page has the same motive. Some rich men are challenged to perpetuate their names. The Methodists formerly had a small school in North Carolina called Trinity College. Mr. Duke gave millions of dollars to that school and they renamed it Duke University in honor of him.

But life's biggest challenge is the challenge that Christ makes to the Christian. What are the challenges of Christ?

I. CHRIST CHALLENGES US TO LIVE A SEPARATED LIFE

He said, "Come ye out from among them." Many Christians have never done this. They do things and go places

49

that are not pleasing to God. This may not hurt them, but it hurts their influence and it certainly hurts the cause of Christ. I wonder if a Christian who knows that he is in the wrong place, a place of sin, ever says to himself, "I claim to be a Christian, but when people see me here, surely they must feel that I am a reproach to the cause of Christ."

A great naturalist was making a study of snakes. He took a poisonous viper, forced its mouth open, inserted a glass under its fangs, and drew out two drops of poison. When he put the poison under a microscope it seemed to contain all the beauties of the rainbow and the aurora borealis. Yet it was deadly poison. Now sin is like that. It looks beautiful and innocent and Christians are often attracted by it. Falling before temptation they go down into the things which hurt themselves, hurt others and the cause of Christ.

The Spaniards have a legend about the petrified man. A certain man who was accused of a crime cried out, "May I turn to stone if I am guilty of this crime." Instantly a miraculous change took place in his body. His arms, his legs, his head and then his entire body turned to stone. Sin will do that to a Christian. His heart will gradually be hardened to the higher and better things of life and he will become deaf and blind to the things of Christ. Someone asked a little girl if she had laid her sins on Jesus. She answered, "Yes, and I don't want to lay any more on Him." Christian, you laid your sins on Jesus when you were saved. Why lay any more on Him? Why not live a separated Christian life?

II. Christ Challenges Us to Live a Faithful Life

Someone asked a Scotch shepherd if his sheep would follow a stranger and he answered, "When they are well they will not do that, but when they are sick they will follow anyone." Why is it that some of Christ's sheep wander from His pasture and into sin and false doctrines? It is because they are sick. They have not been living in the healthful atmosphere of the church and the service of God. When the world calls them they listen and they follow. A pastor's heart aches that he must say of so many people, "I can't count on them and neither can the Lord." I wouldn't be in that class for all the world. How can one be so unfaithful to the Saviour who has been so faithful to him?

> When Jesus came to Golgotha they hanged
> Him on a tree
> They drove great nails through hand and feet,
> And made a Calvary;
> They crowned Him with a crown of thorns,
> red were His wounds and deep,
> For those were crude and cruel days, and human
> flesh was cheap.
>
> When Jesus came to our city, they simply passed
> Him by,
> They never hurt a hair of Him, they only let Him die;
> For men had grown more tender, they would not give
> Him pain,
> They only just passed down the street, and left
> Him in the rain.
>
> Still Jesus cried, "Forgive them for they
> know not what they do,"
> And still it rained the winter rain that
> drenched Him through and through;
> The crowds went home and left the streets without
> a soul to see,
> And Jesus crouched against the wall and cried for
> Calvary.

I wonder if Christ hadn't rather go to Calvary again than to suffer the unfaithfulness of His friends. Surely the cross did not hurt Him as much as our unfaithfulness.

III. Christ Challenges Us to Test Him in Prayer

Over and over He says, "You pray and I will answer and do many wonderful things for you." Listen to *Matthew* 7:7, 8, "Ask and it shall be given you; seek and ye shall find, knock and it shall be opened unto you. For everyone that asketh receiveth; and he that seeketh findeth; and to him that knocketh it shall be opened." Listen also to *Matthew* 18:19, "Again I say unto you, that if two of you shall agree on earth as touching anything that they shall ask, it shall be done for them of my Father which is in heaven."

The trouble with us is that we read about prayer and we know its power, but we do not avail ourselves of this power. Jacob was on the way to meet Esau. He had not seen him since he had cheated him out of his birthright twenty years before that time. He knew that Esau hated him and he was afraid to meet him. So Jacob spent the night in prayer. That's like so many of us. We wait until trouble comes before we feel the need of God.

Back of the lights in our church is a power house, with its tremendous engines and dynamos. Many wires lead out from the power house and into this building. We are told that if we flip a switch that light will fill the building. We test this statement and soon the church is flooded with light. In like manner God says to us, "All of My great power is available to you if you will only pray." And when we test Him in prayer, when we lift our hearts to Him in supplication, light and power from God floods our soul.

A preacher was speaking at a prayer meeting service on the subject, "The Thing That Has Helped Me Most in My Christian Life." A man stood up and said, "The thing that has helped me most in the last ten years is that I have always risen a half hour early in order to spend that time in prayer and Bible study." That is not so unusual, you say. But the man was a street car conductor and this meant that he had to get up at 3 o'clock in the morning. A dear woman in our church ran a boarding house. She also arose at three o'clock in the morning to prepare lunches for her boarders. She spent the first half hour of the day in prayer and in reading her Bible. No wonder everyone looks upon her as a great Christian.

IV. Christ Challenges Us to Bring Our Problems to Him

Every problem can be settled in Christ. I am not saying that He will take the burden away, but I am saying that He will give us grace to bear the burdens. A life boat was pitching about in a heavy storm and the captain cried out, "Hold on, hold on!" Then the voice of a little child came to him, saying, "I can't hold on." Soon she felt the strong arm of the captain about her and she knew that she was safe. There are times when we feel that we cannot hold on, but when we cry out to God we soon feel His arm around us and we know that He will help.

A certain violin-maker in the old days always chose the wood for his violins from the north side of the trees. It was the side that the wind and the storms had beat upon. So he said that in the night when he heard the groaning of the trees in the forest he didn't feel sorry for them, for they were simply learning to be violins. God wants to play sweet music on the strings of our lives, but often we are so full of the world that He can't use us. So He sends trouble or He puts us to bed and we learn His great lessons. Then we are able to glorify Him with our lives.

> What a friend we have in Jesus,
> All our sins and griefs to bear,
> What a privilege to carry
> Everything to God in prayer.
> Oh what peace we often forfeit,
> Oh what needless pain we bear,
> All because we do not carry
> Everything to God in prayer.

Oh let us not try to carry the weight of our burdens alone. He invites us to bring them to Him.

V. Christ Challenges Us to Surrender Our Money for His Use

It is not *our* money, it is all *His*. All that a Christian has belongs to God. If it were not for His help we could never earn a penny. The Bible says that "it is God who giveth thee power to get wealth." Who gives you the breath that you draw? Who gives you the brains and the brawn which make it possible for you to hold down your job? It is God. Now He tells us that at least one-tenth is to be given to His cause. He promises to bless and reward those who tithe.

Years ago in Wichita, Kansas, there was a man named A. A. Hyde. One day he found himself broke and $50,000 in debt. He opened his Bible and read in Genesis how Jacob promised God that he would always tithe if God would bless him. He drew a ring around this verse and he also promised God that he would tithe. A little later a doctor gave him the recipe for a certain ointment. He decided to call this ointment "Mentholatum." This product became very popular and Mr. Hyde became wealthy in a few years. He kept his promise to tithe and soon he was giving far beyond the tithe. I don't claim that God will give you riches if you tithe. I do feel, however, that He will certainly take care of you materially. I hear someone saying, "God is not going to do good things for me simply because I tithe." Well, if you are the Christian that you ought to be, He will. If you don't believe what God says you might as well throw the Bible away. He says that He will bless the tither. I know from personal experience that He will do it, and every faithful tither will testify to the same truth.

The wealthy Baron Rothschild was sitting in a studio, dressed as a beggar. For some reason he wanted his picture taken in that costume. A friend of the artist walked in and saw him sitting there. He thought that the baron was a needy beggar, so he slipped a coin in his hand. The baron accepted the coin and thanked him. Ten years later the man who had made this gift received ten thousand francs from the baron, together with a letter of thanks. So Christ walks through the world today. Often He comes in the garment of a needy soul or of some great cause. So when we give our money in the Name of Christ He does not forget it. He rewards us in this world and in the next.

I wish that I could get every Christian in the world to realize how God would bless him if he faithfully tithed. There is only one way to do it. You must give Him the first tenth, you must give Him His part from the top of your income. You will find then that you have made a great investment for He has said, "Seek ye first the Kingdom of God and His righteousness and all these things shall be added unto you."

VI. Christ Challenges Us to Seek the Lost with Him

Dr. L. R. Scarborough says that a church is "a body of baptized believers going with Christ after the lost." All the work that we do for Him should have one aim in view and that is the winning of the lost to Christ. If this is not true all our work is in vain.

Some years ago on the coast of North Carolina I heard the story of Captain Etheridge of the Coast Guard. A ship was wrecked upon the rocks some distance from the shore. The captain called his men together and they prepared to go out and try to rescue the passengers on the ship. One of his men looked at the dashing waves and said, "Suppose we are not able to get back?" And the captain replied, "We don't have to come back, but we do have to go out and help those people." Oh, I wish that we were just that faithful to our trust. Souls are lost in sin and we must go after them whatever the cost.

VII. Christ Challenges Us to Live a Consecrated Christian Life

This is the sum and substance of the entire challenge. If we are consecrated to Him, we will follow Him and give Him our best. When President Garfield was shot, he was taken to a quiet, isolated house in the country. The railroad planned to run a special track to the house to take doctors and nurses and loved ones to the side of the stricken president. They asked one farmer if they could run the track across his land and he refused. Then they told him it was for the President, and he quickly said, "If it is for President Garfield, you can run the track right through the middle of my house."

Are you willing to give Christ the right-of-way in your life? He may run right through your plans, your engagements and your appointments. It may cost you something. But remember that He said, "If any man will come after Me, let him deny himself, and take up his cross and follow Me."

VIII. WHY OUGHT WE TO ACCEPT CHRIST'S CHALLENGE?

1. *We should accept the challenge for the sake of our own soul's growth.* It is a great joy to know that we are growing in grace. At the end of the year it is good to look back over the months and see that we have experienced some spiritual growth. Some people have been church members for ten or twenty years. They have grown physically, mentally and financially, but they haven't grown an inch spiritually. They know no more of the Bible than they did ten years ago. They give no more, they have no more power in service, they pray no more, they are no more interested in His work. But we thank God for those who can say, "I am not all that I ought to be, I am not all that I am going to be, but I thank God that I am not what I used to be. I have grown some in grace."

2. *We should accept the challenge for the sake of a sinful world.* The world is looking at us. If our religion is a small part of our lives we can never be of any help to them. We must act like we belong to God. We must live lives that are different from the world if we expect to influence and bless the world. When Jacob wrestled all night with the Lord's angel, the angel struck his thigh and Jacob limped the rest of his life. That experience changed him in every way. Christians have had an experience with Christ. As a Christian have you been changed? Can others see Jesus in you?

Often when one has been saved the question is asked, "What was it in the sermon that influenced you?" And the answer came back, "It was not the sermon. It was the good life that someone lived which made me see the beauty of Christianity and my own need of a Saviour."

3. *We should accept the challenge for the sake of Jesus Christ.* We ought to be willing to do anything for Him, for He did everything for us. Yet some of us are not willing to trust Him even with a little money.

Near the railroad station in Fort Worth there once stood a water fountain. It may still be there. On this fountain the following words were engraved, *To the Immortal Honor and Memory of Al Hayne.* There is a story behind this memorial. A building in the city was burning and a woman was trapped on the top floor. There was no way for her to escape. The brave firemen tried to climb the ladders and reach her, but the flames beat them back each time. Suddenly a man rushed out from the crowd, bound his coat about his head and ran up the stairs. He threw that coat around the woman's head, lifted her to his shoulder and made his way down the steps. He laid her on the ground unhurt. Then he staggered back and fell dead. A grateful city erected the fountain in his honor and to his memory.

This man did a great thing for that woman, but Christ did a greater thing for us. He snatched us as brands from the burning. He gave His life that we might live. For His sake let us give our best. Let us accept His challenge. Let us be better Christians.

6.

The Christian's Resources and Responsibilities
Luke 12:48

The text says, "For unto whomsoever much is given, of him shall be much required." This principle runs through all of life. We simply expect more of some than we do of others. This is true of a nation. If a nation is great and strong we expect more from it than from a weak nation. America is a comparatively young Nation, but God has given it the privilege of being the strongest nation in the world. Other nations have a right to expect help from her. We have given that help often. They have re-written the history book in Cuba, leaving out any reference to the help that we have given them. But the fact still remains that in 1898 we came to Cuba's rescue and delivered her from the bondage of Spain. Much has been expected of America and much has been given.

This is also true of families. Much has been given to them and much has been required of them. The Rockefellers and the Fords have made billions, therefore they are expected to give more help than others. So they have set up their big foundations and have given away many millions. This is also true of individuals. If a man has more knowledge and training than someone else, we expect more of him than we do of the other man. If he has greater talents we expect more of him. We expect more of a man who has a good family background of Christian training than we expect of a man who hasn't had this training. We don't expect a steam shovel to do a child's work. We don't expect a mighty organ to give forth tin-whistle sounds. So if a man is more fully endowed than another we expect more of him.

In like manner we expect more of a Christian than of a man who doesn't know Christ as Saviour and Lord. Let us think about what the Christian has been given and what is required of him.

I. What the Christian Has Been Given

1. *He has been given a Saviour.* That is enough to make any man rejoice. It is enough to make any man say, "The God who gave me a Saviour can have all of me." You see, we were lost and on the way to hell. Now that is not a bright prospect. The Bible describes hell as a place of awful suffering and remorse. Some people do not accept that fact, but whether you take this teaching literally or not, we do know that hell is a place of separation from God and a place of conscious suffering.

But God, in His wondrous love, has given us a Saviour to save us from hell. Oh, that is enough to make all the bells of our souls ring with joy. Suppose that you were drowning and going down for the third time, and a man jumped in and saved you. Wouldn't you think that was a pretty wonderful thing? Suppose that you were trapped in a burning building, and a man rescued you and brought you out. Wouldn't you think that to be a pretty wonderful thing? But God did something more wonderful than that when He gave His Only Begotten Son to save you.

One day Jesus sent seventy men out to work and witness for Him. They had a great time. When they came back and made their report, they began to tell that even the devils were subject to them. Then Jesus said to them, "Don't rejoice because you have been able to do these great things. Rejoice because your names are written in heaven." And our names are written in heaven because we have a Saviour. Truly much has been given to us.

2. *He has been given a Bible*. When our loved ones go away, how eagerly we look for their letters! We meet every mail and we are disappointed if we don't get a letter from them. But God never disappoints. He has written a letter called The Bible. It is sweeter than honey in the comb as it tells us of His love for us and as it guides us along the pathway of life.

A lady went to consult a doctor about her health. She poured out a list of symptoms to him, but upon examination he found nothing chronically wrong. "Go home," he said, "and read your Bible an hour every day and come back to me in one month." She was angry at first but finally she decided that this would not hurt her. She had been letting the pleasures of life crowd God out. She came back in a month with her face glowing with health. She said, "I tried your prescription and I am feeling fine. I don't need any more medicine." Then the doctor pointed to the Bible on his desk and said, "If I neglected my daily Bible reading, I would lose the greatest source of strength I have." But here is the pity — God has given us a wonderful book and we neglect it, when all the time it is lying there ready to help us.

3. *He has given us the privilege of prayer*. Every Christian who really prays can count the scores of times when God has miraculously answered his prayers. The trouble with most of us is that we become greatly concerned about something, then we pray about it, and God answers, but we forget to thank Him. Prayer is not always just asking God for something, but it is a submitting of one's self to God. It is a leaving of things in God's hands.

During the war a little war-bride lay in an eastern hospital. Three days before that time she had given birth to a beautiful little girl. But her husband was on the West Coast, waiting to go to the Pacific without seeing the baby. This was pretty hard on the young mother. Then her father came to the bedside and brought the heart-breaking piece of news that the three-day-old baby had to have a serious operation. If the operation was not performed the doctors feared that the baby would die. The young mother took her father's hand and said, "Daddy, don't grieve, my husband and my baby are in God's hand, and I trust Him completely." The baby lived and the husband came safely home, but even if this had not happened she was wise in leaving everything to God. That is one type of prayer and God has given us many answers to our many prayers.

4. *He gives us forgiveness of sin.* Every day we need that, for every day we sin. And every sin stands like a dark cloud between us and God. There is only one way to remove that cloud and we find it in *I John* 1:9, "If we confess our sins, he is faithful and just to forgive us our sins, and to cleanse us from all unrighteousness."

5. *He gives us the promise of heaven.* The child of God is certain of heaven. Nothing can separate him from Christ. Nothing can rob him of his salvation. He is just as sure of heaven the day that he is saved as if he were already inside the gates. At some time all of us get mighty tired, physically, mentally, and even spiritually. We look down the road and we see so many duties piling up before us and so many problems facing us that we wonder if we are going to have strength for it all. We long for rest — we yearn for release from the cares and burdens of life. Well, heaven is going to give us that rest and a thousand things more.

You may have some wonderful days in your life, but the most blessed day is yet to come. It will come to you when you soar up to meet Christ, when you enter into the Pearly Gates, when you see Him face to face. Oh, the glory and bliss that await the Christian! This is another one of God's great gifts.

I don't have space to point out all that God has given and will give us. Even after a million years in eternity we will never be able to recount all of His gifts. From the day that He washed our sins away and throughout eternity God will be giving us every good thing. *James* 1:17 — "Every good gift and every perfect gift is from above and cometh down from the Father."

Now that takes care of the first part of the text, "To whom

much is given." Now let us turn to the second part of the text.

II. What Is Required of a Christian

1. *God requires an undivided heart.* Do you know the trouble with Christians today? They love the Lord a little and the world a lot. They give more allegiance to the things of the world than they do to the things of God. When a man marries a woman he doesn't want her to give him one-tenth of her love and the other nine-tenths to other men. He requires all of it. And God, because of who He is and what He has done for us, requires that our hearts be centered on Him.

There are two voices in every man's soul, the voice of God and the voice of the world. And Satan is behind every worldly voice. Your love for God will determine which voice you will heed. God has a right to ask you to love Him above everything else on earth.

2. *God requires a holy life.* By "a holy life" I do not mean a perfect life, but I do mean that in every way every day you try to live a consecrated, separated, dedicated Christian life. We don't influence people so much by what we say or how we look, but we influence them tremendously by the way we live every day.

Dr. G. Campbell Morgan was pastor of a church in London. A young man came to him and told him that he had been living a dissipated life and that now he wanted to become a Christian. He was received into the church and didn't miss a single service for several months. Then he dropped out of the church and Dr. Morgan went to see him. He said to him, "I have come to tell you how much we have been missing you here at the church." And the young man said, "There is no use for you to talk to me about your Christianity. I have tried it and it's a failure." Then Dr. Morgan seized a number of lewd pictures on the mantle and threw them into the fire, saying as he did it, "How can you ever expect to be a real Christian unless you burn your bridges behind you?" O Christian, God expects you to burn all of your bridges behind you and live a life that is pleasing to Him. He has given you so much. He has a right to expect this of you.

3. *God requires active service.* It is not enough to be good, you must do good. A man moved into our city and came to our church. He had been active in a church of another city but felt that he could let up on his work here. In a sermon I said, "In the Lord's work if you try to rest you will rust." This man got the point, soon plunged into the work and now is one of the happiest men in our church.

Dr. Winfred Moore tells about a boy in England who was taken to church by his nurse the first time when he was seven years of age. The preacher opened a big book and began to talk about a man named Jesus. He told about how Jesus went about doing good and how He was mistreated and finally put upon a cross. The boy was greatly moved and whispered to his nurse, "Why don't these men do something about this? Why do they let Him die?" The nurse said, "You mustn't talk in church." As soon as church was over he said to her, "Why don't they go now and do something about this good man who is being mistreated?" And the nurse replied, "You mustn't talk about these things. People will think that you are odd."

Oh, my friends, we do need to do something about it. We couldn't save Him from the cross, but we can serve Him. Let the world call us "odd." Let us be willing to be fools for Christ's sake. He has done so much for us. It is required of us that we serve Him.

4. *God expects a faithful stewardship.* God has entrusted us with all that we have. We must use it rightfully for Him. In this sermon I want to discuss with you the stewardship of money. I know that some people object when a preacher talks about money. They say that he ought to preach the Gospel. Let me tell you that this is a vital part of it. The Bible says more about money than it does about heaven and hell. God wants you to do well financially, so He lays down a rule for giving in His Book. He says that if you bring the tithe into His storehouse, He will pour

out such blessings that you will not have room enough to receive them. And every faithful tither will tell you that God keeps His promise.

Recently I went into a very luxurious home. The furniture was elegant, the rugs deep and soft, the pictures beautiful and expensive. They had two cars in the garage and the back and front yards were filled with beautiful shrubbery. I was glad for these people to have such a nice home until I remembered that they were giving the Lord only ten dollars per month. Then I felt ashamed for them before the Lord. The majority of Christians are not as well fixed as that family. They have the necessities of life, but not many luxuries. They are the ones who need to tithe more than the rich people. They need it because God promises to take care of them if they tithe. They need it in order that their souls might grow.

Some years ago a man offered $25,000 to any one who faithfully practiced tithing and could truly say that God had not blessed him. No one ever claimed the money. This man was simply banking on the fact that God would keep His promise. I have seen many people start out the year by giving God His tithe. In a month or two they wanted something for themselves and so they quit tithing. Soon things were going badly with them. What was the trouble? They were simply not giving God a chance to bless them. They were not taking Him at His word. But every faithful tither can say, "God keeps His word. You will never lack anything if you go His way." The reason so many people do not tithe is because they are afraid that they will not be able to get along financially. Oh, can't you trust God? He is not bankrupt. He will take care of you.

So I challenge you to test God. When you get your next pay envelope, put aside one tenth for Him. I promise you that He will not fail you. Much has been given you, at least a tenth is required.

5. *God expects us to witness for Him.* You had a dread disease called sin, but you found Christ to be the remedy.

Others are dying with this same disease, don't you owe it to them to tell them of the remedy?

Mr. H. C. Coleman was a successful business man who donated thousands of dollars to Hardin Simmons University. One time he invited the president of the University, Dr. Sandifer, to go with him on a trip to California in his car. They had a pleasant time. One day Mr. Coleman had the chauffeur stop at a florist's shop to purchase some flowers. Dr. Sandifer wondered what he was going to do with the flowers, but he said nothing. The journey was resumed and soon the chauffeur stopped the car beside a cemetery on a hill. Mr. Coleman asked Dr. Sandifer to wait for him. He then took the flowers, walked up the hill, and put them on a lonely grave. Then he stood there with his head bared in prayer for a long time. When he came back to the car, Dr. Sandifer said to him, "Is a member of your family buried there?" And Mr. Coleman answered, "No, an old lady by the name of Mrs. Smith lies buried there. Once she lived in Philadelphia and ran a little mission there. I was a wayward boy on the streets and she invited me in and led me to know Jesus Christ as my Saviour. I never come to California but that I put some flowers on her grave in gratitude for what she did for me." Oh, when life's little day is over for you, will anyone be able to say, "You told me about Jesus and now I am a Christian"?

Yes, much has been given to us and much is required. God has given us great resources and we have great responsibilities. Come with me to a lonely hill called Calvary. On a cross on the top of that hill the Saviour is dying. You and I belong on that cross, but He took our place. He has a message for us. What is He saying? He is saying, "I am dying here for you. I am doing this to save you and keep you out of hell. I am shedding My blood to cover your sins. I am opening up the way to heaven for you." Oh, in the light of that sacrifice, how can we help but bow our heads and say, "Lord, from now on you can have my very best."

I gave My life for thee,
My precious blood I shed,
That thou might'st ransomed be,
And quickened from the dead.
I gave, I gave My life for thee,
What hast thou given for Me?

7.

Don't Settle for One Without the Other
Ezekiel 47:1-5

A certain man traveled aboard a great ocean liner going
from London to New York. Day after day he ate cheese
and crackers. At lunch time on the last day out, one of
the ship's officers found him sitting in one of the deck chairs
eating his lunch of cheese and crackers. The officer asked
him, "Why don't you go into the ship's dining room and eat
with the other passengers?" And the man replied, "I can't
afford it." "Why man," said the officer, "you paid for those
meals when you bought your ticket! It wouldn't have cost
you anything to eat your meals on this ship." There are
many Christians like this. They are satisfied with so little
when God offers so much. They are satisfied to get their
names on a church roll book and let it go at that. But God
offers much more than that. He has great happiness and joy
and usefulness for those who go deeper with Him.

Look at our text from the Book of Ezekiel. The prophet
says that in a vision he saw a man leading him out from the
temple and he saw water running out from the temple.
As the man and he walked along the man measured off a
distance of a thousand cubits and the water was up to the
ankles. He measured another thousand cubits and the
water was up to the knees. He measured another thousand
and the water was up to the loins. Finally the waters became a river that could not be passed over, waters to swim in.

Now this is a picture of Christians today. Some of them

come to Christ, but they never go any deeper than ankle depth. Their religion means little to them. Some go a little deeper, up to knee-depth. Some go deeper still, up to loin-depth. Then a few of them go all the way with God. They swim in the love and service and power of a great God.

In this message I want to urge you to go all the way with God. Don't be content with second best. "Don't settle for one without the other."

I. Don't Settle for Salvation Without Assurance

It is wonderful to be saved. It is more wonderful to know it. And the Bible tells us plainly that we can know it. Paul knew it. Listen to him as he says, "I know whom I have believed and am persuaded that He will keep that which I have committed unto Him against that day." There was no doubt in him and there need to be no doubt in us. One of our men was talking the other day to a preacher in our city. This preacher said, "I don't know whether I am going to heaven or not. I will have to wait until I die and then see whether or not I get into the gates of glory." Now how much help and hope and comfort could such a man have and how could he help anyone else?

Now we know how a man is saved. He is not saved because of his works. Yet most of the religions of the world teach that salvation is based on works. I was in Hawaii sometime ago and while the other members of my party went into a curio shop I drifted across the street into a little church of a well-known denomination. I picked up a tract in the church which plainly stated that baptism was the way into the Kingdom of God. That is salvation by works. You can work twenty-four hours a day for God and others, you can pile up your good deeds, you can give a fortune to the church, and still be forever lost. These things cannot wash away a single sin.

No, our salvation rests in the person of Jesus Christ. We become children of God when we face up to the fact that we are sinners and when we turn from our sins and in simple child-like faith we trust Christ for spiritual life, even as we trust the doctor for physical life when we go to the operating room.

Sometime ago the wife of one of our deacons brought a woman to my office. She said, "My friend here is going to the hospital for surgery tomorrow and she wants to be saved." As I talked to the lady, she told me of the churches which she had attended as a child. I told her to forget about these churches and think of Christ and her own personal need. She told me that she had great confidence in the doctor who was going to operate on her. I told her to come in simple repentance and faith to Christ, trusting Him as she was trusting her doctor. After we had prayed and talked together, she was soon rejoicing in Christ as her Saviour. You can see, then, that our salvation involves an experience with the Lord Jesus Christ.

All the salvation scriptures center in Christ.

> *John* 1:12 — "But as many as received him to them gave he the power to become the sons of God, even to them that believe on his name."
>
> *John* 6:37 — "All that the Father giveth me shall come to me; and him that cometh to me I will in no wise cast out."
>
> *Matthew* 10:32 — "Whosoever therefore shall confess me before men, him will I confess also before my Father which is in heaven."
>
> *Romans* 10:13 — "For whosoever shall call upon the name of the Lord shall be saved."
>
> *John* 3:16 — "For God so loved the world that he gave his only begotten son, that whosoever believeth in him should not perish, but have everlasting life."

Now how can we know that we are saved? We know that we are saved if we have carried out the instructions of the Word. If we have repented of our sins, trusted Christ as our Saviour, confessed Him and given ourselves over to

Christ, we can know that we are saved, because He said that we would be and He never lies.

We know that we are saved by our changed attitude toward the world. Do you love the things of God or the things of the world? What satisfies you, the things of Christ or worldly things? Which had you rather attend, a revival service or a night club? A preacher met one of his members on Monday morning and said to him, "I heard that you went to the ball game yesterday instead of attending church." And the man replied, "That's a lie, and I have the fish to prove it." You can see what satisfied him.

One thing puzzles me greatly. Why is it that so many people who have joined the church never attend, never give and seem to have no interest in spiritual things? Maybe the answer is right here. Maybe they have never been saved. I don't see how any saved person could stay away from the things of God.

We know that we are saved if we love the brethren. The Bible says, "We know that we have passed from death unto life because we love the brethren." And Jesus said, "By this shall all men know that ye are My disciples, because ye have love one for the other."

We know that we are saved because of the witness of the Spirit. His Spirit bears witness with our spirit, that we are the children of God. When I hear a certain song or a sermon that is full of Christ, something within me makes a ready response. My spirit goes out to meet the spirit of God and I know that I belong to Him. If you have been saved, if you belong to God, there is a rapport between God and you which makes you know that you are His child. You feel Him within and you sing, "It's real, praise God, I know it's real."

Dwight L. Moody said, "I have never known a Christian who was any good in the work of Christ who did not have the assurance of salvation." Certainly this is true. How can you serve God and lead others to Christ if you are not sure of Him yourself? So let me say, "Don't settle for salvation without assurance. Go to the Bible, go to your knees. Be sure that you are a child of God, then live like it."

II. Don't Settle for Conversion Without a Vital Church Connection

I have heard people say, "I am a Christian. I have been saved, but I am not a member of any church." All the world has a right to doubt your salvation. Church membership is not a part of the plan of salvation, but it is definitely a part of Christ's plan for your life. He put the church here for His people to live in and serve through. He knew human nature, He knew that the Christian would need a spiritual home, a place where he could get his spiritual batteries recharged, a place where he could tie his soul up like a ship being tied up to the dock. Therefore He gave us the church, the most wonderful institution in the world.

I am called on to preach many funerals. The funeral director often calls me to conduct the funeral of someone of whom I have never heard. When I ask if the deceased has been a church member, I am often told, "Yes, he was a member of the church, but he has lived here forty years without moving his membership." If a person has no more interest in the church which God set up for him down here in the world, then the world has a right to wonder if this person ever knew the Saviour. I believe that if you are a real Christian and realize what Christ has done for you, nothing can keep you out of the church.

Hebrews 10:25 — "Not forsaking the assembling of ourselves together, as the manner of some is; but exhorting one another; and so much the more as we see the day approaching." What is the inspired writer saying here? He is saying that Christ is coming again and that we ought to be faithful to His church. I would hate to meet Him and be forced to say, "Lord, You saved me, but I never did line up with Your church." The Great Commission says that we are to go into all the world and tell men of Christ. You can't do that by yourself, but you can join with others and send the message of Christ to all the world. If you are not in the church, you have no part in obeying that command. The Bible tells us to bring all of our tithes into the storehouse of God. Where can you bring them if you are not in the church? The Bible tells us to "come into His courts with thanksgiving." If people didn't join a church and build buildings and furnish services we couldn't come together in His courts for worship. The Bible tells us to "study to show thyself approved unto God." The place of study is furnished by the church. You just can't carry out the great commands of Christ unless you are in the church.

Are you a Christian? Are you out of the church? Then you will have no influence for Christ. Go and try to win someone to Him and they will ask you, "Of what church are you a member?" When you tell them that you are not a member of a church, they will not listen to you further. They will have no confidence in your religion. So don't settle for conversion without a vital church connection.

III. Don't Settle for Eternal Life Without Holy Living

Someone says, "I have been once saved and once saved means always saved. I am on the way to heaven, so it doesn't matter very much how I live." Oh, yes it does, it matters tremendously. I can't think of a sorrier ingrate in the world than a man who lets Christ save him and who then goes out to live for the devil. It matters to you as to how you live. If there is a spark of God within you, you can't be happy while you are living an unholy life. You may forget the matter for a while, but the time will come when you will say, "O God, I am miserable. I know that I am not living as I should."

Then it matters to others as to how you live. One of our evangelistic singers says that one day his little boy was playing in the yard with some other boys. He overheard their conversation. One little boy said, "My dad knows the mayor of the city." Another little boy said, "My dad knows the governor." Then the singer's boy said, "That's nothing, my dad knows God." How can other people know that we know God if we don't live for Him?

Then it matters to God as to how you live. His richest blessings are for those who live faithfully for Him. And His reward at the end of the way depends upon your life for Him. Oh, may God help you to say, "He has saved me and blessed me, therefore I must live a good life for Him."

IV. Don't Settle for Receiving Without Giving

It is indeed more blessed to give than to receive, but too many people say, "Oh well, receiving is good enough for me." And they lose the greater blessing. What can a Christian give as he remembers what Christ has given him? He can give his time, he can give his talents, he can give his service, he can give his money.

Now everyone can give Him some money. You may not have great talents to be used for Him, but if you have any income at all, you can give Him His tithe. You notice that I have said, "His tithe." It is His, and you have no right to use it for yourself. There are some fine men in our church who can't teach a class, who can't sing a solo, who can't lead in public prayer, but they do give their money to the cause of Christ.

How much should a man give unto the Lord? The Bible tells us that we ought to give Him one-tenth of our income, then when we are able we ought to make a love offering beyond that. And God never lets a man suffer who lives for Him and gives what God tells him to give. He provides every need and gives many extras over and above.

Dr. J. D. Grey of New Orleans met a five-year-old boy on the way to Sunday school. The boy was crying and Dr. Grey asked why he was crying. The boy's mother told the preacher that the boy had spent his allowance and now had nothing to put in the offering plate. Dr. Grey said to the boy, "I will make you a proposition. I will lend you a nickel to put in the offering and you can pay me back later." The boy stopped crying, his face lighted up and he accepted the loan. He marched into the church happy that he could make an offering. The next week the preacher received a letter saying, "Dear Dr. Grey, I am sorry I haven't seen you this week. I am paying my debt to you, five cents. Thank you very much." Did you ever weep because you couldn't give anything to the Lord? I wish that all of our people were just as concerned about their giving to God as was this little boy.

There is joy in giving. Don't be content just to take everything in and give nothing out. You are not living until you are giving.

V. Don't Settle for Heaven Without a Crown

Jesus said, "Lay not up for yourselves treasures on earth, where rust corrupts and thieves break through and steal, but lay up treasures in heaven." How can you lay up treasures in heaven? You can't send God a personal check. But you can invest your lives and your money in the things of God, and then He will put that to your credit in glory.

There is no crown in heaven for those who come up empty-handed. The rewards are for those who have faithfully served Him. A Christian woman says that when she was a little girl her mother called her early one morning and said, "Honey, I am sick this morning. Will you get up and get father's breakfast?" She quickly answered, "Yes, mother." She meant to do it, but instead she turned over and went back to sleep. The mother got up and prepared breakfast. The little girl didn't realize how sick the mother was. She died a few days later. This woman said that for many years she had carried with her the sad memory of how she had failed her mother in the time of need.

I am afraid that many of us who get to heaven will carry

with us some sad memories also. God needed us and the church needed us, but we were too occupied with our own ease and pleasures. And when we meet the Man with the nail prints in His hands, we are going to be sorry that we failed Him. Oh, don't be content just to get into heaven. Give God your best here and He will give you His best here and hereafter.

8.

The Best Thing That Can Be Said About a Christian

I Corinthians 4:1-5

What is the best thing that can be said about a Christian, a follower of Christ? "He comes to church." Now that is a good thing to be said about a Christian, but that is the least he can do. That is not the best thing you can say about him. "He is active in the Lord's service." Every Christian ought to be on the job for the Lord, but this is not the best thing you can say about him. "He lives a clean life." That is good. If a man is a Christian, it ought to show up in his life, but that is not the best thing you can say about him. "He stands up for what is right." A Christian ought to take a stand for the right, but that is not the best thing you can say about him. "He gives his money generously." Every Christian ought to give at least a tithe and many should go farther than that, but that is not the best thing you can say about him.

The best thing you can say about a Christian is that he is faithful. If he is faithful in every way, he will do all of these other things. Jesus said, "Be thou faithful unto death." Paul said, "It is required in stewards, that a man be found faithful." Men may compliment you in many ways, but when they say that you are a faithful man, faithful to the Lord and His church and to the highest things in life, they are paying you the highest compliment that you can ever receive.

I. FIRST, LET US THINK OF THE FAITHFULNESS OF OTHERS

1. *God is faithful.* All the way through the Bible you hear man proclaiming the faithfulness of God. Then we

76

hear Jeremiah crying out, "Great is Thy faithfulness." God is faithful to His creation. Look at the way that the sun and the moon and the earth revolve, bringing night and day and all the four seasons. When you go to bed at night, you don't have to worry about another day coming in the morning. You don't fear that the night will be six months long. You know that a faithful God is running the universe.

And oh, how faithful God is to us. He is faithful to save us, faithful to provide our needs, faithful to answer our prayers, faithful to forgive our sins and to cleanse us from all unrighteousness. He is faithful in life, faithful in death, faithful always. We are fickle and spasmodic. We are true one day and false the next, but God is always faithful. He is "the same yesterday, today and forever." We would not be here today if it were not for the faithfulness of God. I know scores of people who were formerly very faithful. They never missed a church service. They lived faithfully for the Lord. But today they have no concern for the church nor for the things of God. They are not faithful to God, yet God continues to be faithful to them in spite of their disloyalty.

2. *Jesus is faithful.* I see Him as He goes down to the Jordan River and is baptized of John. I see Him dying on the cross. And all the way in between these two events He was faithful. He came into the world with one supreme purpose in His heart. He came to die for the sins of men. He set His face toward the cross and never wavered. He never turned to the right nor to the left. He was faithful unto death.

An artist has painted a picture of Christ as a boy. He is in the carpenter's shop and the sun is sinking into the west. He goes to the window and stretches out His arms, thus casting a shadow behind Him. It is the shadow of a cross. That shadow never left Him. He remained faithful to His destiny. He kept straight ahead until the cross claimed Him. He was faithful to the Father, He was faithful to His friends, He was faithful to the world for which He bled and died.

3. *The disciples were faithful.* It is believed that only one of them lived to die a natural death. They gave up their lives rather than be unfaithful to Christ. It is so easy to be a Christian today. No one will shoot you for coming to church or tear you limb from limb for following Christ. Yet they endured all of these things and still kept faithful. I wonder how our people could stand the test today. Suppose that a man came to you and said, "I hold in my hand a million dollars. I also have a gun. If you renounce Christ I will give you your life and a million dollars. If you remain true to Him, I will kill you. Take your choice." I wonder how many of us would remain faithful to Him under these circumstances.

4. *Others have been faithful.* I was talking to a man the other day about a doctor who was a devoted Christian and faithful member of our church. When this man asked about the doctor, I said, "He is faithful in everything, he stands up for what he thinks is right and he is generous in his giving. He is a consecrated Christian." And the man replied, "Yes, he is all of that and I admire him for it." I don't think this man is a faithful church member, but he admires the man who is.

So as we look at God and Christ and the disciples and some modern Christians, we are exhorted also to plant our feet in the pathway of loyalty.

II. Different Motives for Faithfulness

1. *One man says, "I am going to be loyal in order to get something from God."* That is the lowest motive. Jacob is our example here. He left home a poor man, running away from his brother's wrath. The first night out he slept under the stars. He had a wonderful dream that night. He saw a ladder reaching from earth to heaven, with the angels going up and down on that ladder, and God Himself standing at the top. When he awoke the next morning, he said, "God surely is in this place. I am going to make a bargain with Him." So Jacob said, "Lord, if You go with me and protect me and bless me, I will give You a

tenth of all that I make." Now that is the wrong motive. All Christians ought to tithe. They are robbing God when they don't. But we are not to tithe for what we get out of it. We are not to tithe, expecting God to pay us back with interest. We are to tithe because it is right and because we love God and we want to do that which is right.

Here is the truth about the tithe. Abraham commenced it, Moses commanded it, Jesus commended it, so who am I to cancel it? I know that God does bless the tither. I know that from my own experience and from the experience of others. But we are not to give or serve simply because we think that by so doing we will get something from God.

2. *Another motive — to be loyal because of what God has done for you.* This is not a bad motive, but it is not the best. David is our example here. He said in *Psalm* 116:12, "What shall I render unto the Lord for all of His benefits toward me?" He was simply saying, "The Lord has been good to me, so I know that I owe Him something in return." That is true enough, but we are not to treat God's goodness as a debt. We are not to say, "God did this for me, so I must pay Him back."

Now when you sit down and think of all that the Lord has done for you, you can't pass it off lightly. He lifted us up out of the miry clay, set our feet upon a rock, redeemed our souls and placed our feet on the road to heaven. Don't you feel that you owe Him something?

> Were the whole realm of nature mine,
> That were a present far too small,
> Love so amazing, so divine,
> Demands my soul, my life, my all.

3. *Another motive — "I will be loyal in spite of anything that happens to me."* This is the highest motive. Job was a rich man. He had a fine family, his cup of happiness overflowed. Then in one fell swoop he lost everything. He lost his children, he lost his money, he lost his health. You know how painful it is to have one boil somewhere on your body, but Job had them from the crown of his head to the sole of his feet. Yonder he sits on the ash-heap

and his wife comes out to see him. Does she bring soothing ointment for his sores? No, just listen to her. "Job, you are a fool. You have been loyal to God and look what it got you. You are penniless now. Your children are gone. You are sick all over. What kind of a God is He, anyway? Why don't you curse Him and die?" Now this mighty man shows his true loyalty. We hear him saying, "Though He slay me, yet will I trust Him." That is real loyalty, a loyalty which says, "In spite of everything, I will be loyal to my God."

That is the kind of loyalty we need today. Too many people let little things sweep them off their feet. No matter what happens or what anyone says or does, we ought to be true to Christ in spite of it. So you don't like the preacher, so the church is not run to suit you, so someone talked about you, so your Sunday school class elected someone else to the position you felt you deserved. What of it? You must be loyal to God in spite of these things.

Peter was talking to Jesus just before His ascension. He pointed to John and said, "Lord, what plans do you have for John?" And Jesus answered, "What is that to thee, follow thou Me." So whatever happens we are to be loyal to Christ. We are to follow Him in spite of all the troubles of life.

III. How Can We Show Our Loyalty?

1. *By consecrated, consistent Christian living.* The spasmodic off-and-on Christian will never have any influence for Christ. You must be a twenty-four-hour-a-day, three hundred and sixty-five days a year Christian to have any influence for the Lord. Maybe you can't speak in public or sing a solo. Maybe you can't give huge sums. But there is one thing you can do. You can live such a good life that every day people will see Jesus in you. Many a person has gone to hell because they watched the life of an inconsistent, unfaithful Christian. Many a person has come to Christ and gone to heaven because they could not get away from the power of a consecrated, faithful Christian life.

2. *By standing up for our convictions.* This is sorely needed today. We believe in certain things when we are in church on Sunday. Are we willing to stand up for these beliefs before the world during the week?

We do not hand out a set of rules to our people and say, "You must do this and not do that." No, we leave each member to live by the Spirit of Christ and the teachings of the Bible. We say to our people, "Read the Bible for yourself. Pray about everything. Live up to the spirit as well as to the law of the Gospel." We don't force anyone to do anything, but we do urge our people to stand up for their convictions.

3. *By our obedience.* The next step after salvation is obedience, obedience in baptism, obedience in having a vital church connection, obedience in doing all that Christ has commanded.

A certain man was given the task of distributing salvation tracts. No one seemed to appreciate him so he became discouraged and gave up the work. Twenty years later he met a man who had been saved through a tract that he had given out on the last day that he worked. That man was busy for the Lord, giving out salvation tracts. The first man said to him, "I have let you take my crown." Oh, if you receive a crown of glory it will be because you were obedient.

On January 19, 1879, Tom MacKay was asked to stand outside of the Pacific Garden Mission in Chicago and invite people in to the services. It was a cold, snowy night. A stiff wind was blowing in off Lake Michigan. He said to himself, "No one will be out on a night like this. I think I will go in where it is warm." Then he thought for a moment and said, "No, I was asked to stand here and I will do it." Soon he noticed a man shuffling down the street. He invited that man into the mission and the man was saved. Who was that man? It was Mel Trotter, founder of the City Rescue Mission of Grand Rapids and a most successful evangelist. Yes, something happens when we are faithful and obedient to Christ.

4. *By loyalty to His church.* In *I Corinthians* 3 Paul speaks of the rewards in heaven. He plainly teaches us that the works we do for the world will be burned up at the judgment. The works that we have done for Christ and His church will bring a rich reward. Yet so many Christians are giving their lives to the things which do not count for God. I watched a certain couple who were members of my church. They were faithful to every service. They were active in the work of the Lord. Then they let the world creep in. They began to play golf on Sunday afternoon and that kept them from coming to the Sunday night service. They had supper at the Country Club on Wednesday night, and that kept them from coming to prayer meeting. Soon they were attending church just once in a while on Sunday morning. Before long they were doing things that they never would have thought of doing otherwise. You can say what you will about your church, but God has put something there to help you in your life if you are faithful and loyal to Him.

5. *By witnessing for Christ.* Dr. Leo Eddleman has likened the soul-winner to a pilot light on the stove. You don't use the pilot light to cook anything with, but you use it to start up a bigger flame. Spurgeon was a mighty preacher, and the whole world knows his name. But no one knows the name of the humble layman who preached one Sunday morning and pointed his finger at young Spurgeon, saying, "Look to Jesus, young man." This layman was just a pilot light, but look at the flame that he kindled. Andrew is a little known man of the Bible, but everyone knows his big brother, Simon Peter. But Andrew was the pilot light. He brought his big brother to Jesus.

One Sunday afternoon a group of baseball players walked down a street in Chicago. They heard music coming from a mission station. A woman came over and invited them to come to the services at the mission. All of them laughed except one fellow by the name of Billy Sunday. He said to the other baseball players, "You can go wherever you want to, I am going to this service." He heard the Gospel and was saved and became a flaming evangelist. What was the name of the woman? We do not know, but God knows. She was the pilot light which lighted the flame of salvation in Billy Sunday's heart.

6. *By giving God the glory in all things.* The greatest temptation of the Christian worker comes right here. It is so easy to claim credit for ourselves, when all the glory should go to God. I doubt if any of us ever accomplishes anything for God without help from some other source. Paul had the idea when he said, "I have planted, Apollos watered, but God gave the increase." And God ought to have the glory for all that we do.

One day every Christian shall stand before the judgment seat of Christ. There his works will be judged and the rewards given out. Up steps a famous preacher, one whose name was upon thousands of lips and whose sermons turned many to Calvary. The judge examines the record and says, "Well done, thou good and faithful servant, enter thou into the joys of thy Lord." Then up comes a little old lady. She is no longer old, for she is robed with eternal youth. Is there any use for her to stand before the judge? Can she expect any reward? She lived in poverty and when she died, very few people even took notice of the fact. But the judge examines the record and when he reads of her faithfulness, he says to her as he said to the great preacher, "Well done, thou good and faithful servant, enter into the joys of thy Lord." They were unlike in talents, but alike in faithfulness, so they received a like reward. Faithfulness is the basis of our rewards in heaven.

Some years ago at the Olympic Games in Sweden a young Indian named Jim Thorpe excelled in every contest. The King of Sweden presented the medal and said, "You are the greatest amateur athlete in the world today." This made the young man very happy. But back in America it was discovered that one summer he had accepted pay for playing on a village baseball team. This disqualified him as an amateur and he had to send his trophies back to Sweden with a letter apologizing for what he had done, even though it broke his heart. But, thank God, if we strive lawfully for Christ we will win a crown that we can never lose.

What then shall we do with our crown? Dr. H. A. Ironside answers the question for us. One day he preached about crowns and rewards. A woman came up to him afterward and said, "Am I to understand that you are working for a reward and looking forward to a crown?" And the great preacher said, "Yes, I am." "Well," she said, "I am disappointed in you. I thought you labored out of pure love for Christ and not for a reward." "But," said Dr. Ironside, "remember what I said we are to do with our crowns. We are to cast them at Jesus' feet." "Oh," she said, "I hadn't thought of that."

May God help us to be faithful so that when we come to the end of the way we will have some crowns to lay down at the feet of Him who loved us and gave Himself for us.

> All hail the power of Jesus' Name,
> Let angels prostrate fall,
> Bring forth the royal diadem,
> And crown Him Lord of all.

9.

Giants, Grasshoppers and God
Numbers 13:17-33

This is a story of tragedy and failure. It is a story of unbelief on the part of ten men and faith on the part of two men. It is a story of a people who saw the Promised Land, but who were afraid to enter into it. This story applies to modern times, for today there are thousands who come up to the Promised Land, look in for a time and then turn back into the wilderness.

God's people, Israel, had been in slavery in Egypt. He heard their cries of distress and sent Moses to lead them out and into Canaan. Now, after days of toil and trouble, they come to the border of the Promised Land. God was ready for them to go in and find homes in the land flowing with milk and honey. So Moses picked out twelve men and sent them in to spy out the land. They stayed there for forty days, then they returned and made their report. They brought back many trophies from the land, proving that it was all God said it was. Why, it took two men to carry one cluster of grapes found in that wonderful country.

Let us listen to the majority report of the first ten men. They said, "It is indeed a wonderful country. All that we need is there, but the people look like giants and they live in strong cities. We could never overcome them. We were just like grasshoppers in their sight." Then Caleb and Joshua stood up. "Mr. Chairman," one of them said. "We would like to bring a minority report. Truly it is a wonderful land. It is true that the men there look like giants. But God is with us and with His help we can go in and possess the land."

But the people were afraid and their faith was weak. So they said, "We can't go in. It would be suicide to try. It would be better for us if we had stayed in Egypt and been slaves all of our lives." Then God spoke. "All right," He said, "because you have no faith and because you would not follow My leadership, I will let you go back into the wilderness. You will be forced to wander there for forty years. Not one of those twenty years or older will even enter the Promised Land except Caleb and Joshua. These men put their faith in Me and were willing to go with Me against the giants."

Now let us learn some lessons at Kadesh-Barnea!

I. There Is the Kadesh - Barnea of Salvation

Men come to the point where they must decide for Christ and heaven or Satan and hell. They stand there and look into the Promised Land. All the joys of Christ await over there. But on the other side of the line they see the world. Its delights beckon them. They are urged to continue in the wilderness. They are at the borderline now. They can go into the land and know Christ and live useful lives for God, or they can turn their back on Christ, live meaningless lives and sink at last into eternal death.

I may be speaking to someone who is not a Christian. You believe that the Christian life is the only life to live, you believe that one day you must account for that life at the Judgment. You know that it is best for time and eternity to be a Christian. Some day you expect to make your decision, but you keep putting it off. It may be that this morning you are standing at Kadesh-Barnea. You must make the decision now. Will you go over into the Promised Land or remain in the wilderness of sin and unbelief?

In the days of the crusades an Englishman named Gilbert Beckett was captured by a Saracen King and used as a slave. The time came when the king's daughter fell in love with the young Englishman. When the king learned about this love affair he released Gilbert and sent him back to England. The girl began to fail in health. The doctors could not help her. She longed to see the one whom she loved and finally decided to go to England and find him. She wrote her father a note and set sail for England. She knew only two English words, "London" and "Gilbert." She found her way from port to port by using the word "London." Finally she arrived in London but no one there could understand her language except the one word "Gilbert." She went up and down the streets speaking just that one word. The people thought she had lost her mind. Then one day a servant from Gilbert's house saw her and heard her crying out, "Gilbert." He knew the story, so he led her to Gilbert's house where they had a very happy reunion. They were later married and she became the mother of Thomas a Beckett, the famous martyr.

Two words brought triumph and happiness to the Saracen maid. They were "Gilbert" and "London." But there are two words greater than these. They are "Jesus" and "Calvary." So I beg you not to stay in the wilderness but to cross over Kadesh-Barnea and come to Calvary. Breathe there the name of Christ in faith and the Promised Land will open up for you.

II. There Is the Kadesh - Barnea of Temptation

Every man is tempted, both those who live closest to God and those who follow Him afar off. You come to the point of decision and are tempted to give in. Temptation is real and fascinating. You look down the pathway of sin and your feet want to go that way.

But there is an Upper Road. It is the road of self-denial, the road of hardness and discipline. It is so easy to yield to sin and so hard to say "No" to temptation. This means a crucifixion of our appetites and our sinful desires. But there is help for you on that Upper Road. Jesus is there. He knows all about temptation and He can help you.

> Take the Name of Jesus with you
> As a shield from every snare,
> When temptations round you gather,
> Breathe that Holy Name in prayer.

When you stand at the Kadesh-Barnea of temptation, you can go one of two ways. You can go over into the land where Christ stands to help you, or you can sink into the wilderness of sin.

III. There Is the Kadesh - Barnea of Consecration

Oh, so many Christians come to this borderline! They look over the line and see all the joys and usefulness that are in a life of consecration. But they see that it will cost them something, so they turn away from a life of consecration and wander in the wilderness of a meaningless life. You look at some wonderful Christian and when you see how radiantly happy he is and how God uses him, you say, "Oh, I wish I could be like that." But you are not willing to pay the price.

You read these words in *Galatians* 2:20, "I am crucified with Christ; nevertheless I live, yet not I, but Christ liveth in me: and the life which I now live in the flesh I live by the faith of the Son of God, who loved me, and gave himself for me." Then you say, "I wish that were true of me. I wish that I could be completely consecrated to Christ."

Then you read *Romans* 12:1, "I beseech you therefore, brethren, by the mercies of God, that ye present your bodies a living sacrifice, holy, acceptable unto God, which is your reasonable service." And right there you stand at Kadesh-Barnea. God is urging you to cross over into a consecrated Christian life and the world is calling you to be a half-way Christian. Oh, that the Lord would stir men's hearts to a full surrender to Him.

Rev. William Pennefeather, a great Christian of England, walked down the street with a friend. A beggar approached them and looked for a moment into the face of the other man. Then he looked into the face of William Pennefeather and said, "Oh, man with heaven in your face, give me a penny." Maybe you have met someone with heaven in his face or her face and you have longed to have heaven in your face, too. You were on the borderline for a moment. What is your decision? Will you go the way of consecration or the way of the world?

IV. There Is the Kadesh - Barnea in the Home

You have a home with your children about you. You realize that God has placed a tremendous responsibility upon you. You want to rear these children for God. You want them to live so as to bring a blessing to you and the world. You look in upon another family and you see how closely knit they are. You see how much love is there. You see how happy they are. If you look closely you will see that the parents are dedicated Christians. They are bringing their children up in the fear and admonition of the Lord. They don't send them to church, they go with them. They don't spend their time for the world, they give time to their children and to God. It seems that the father and the mother and the children are just walking along with Christ.

Then you say, "That's the kind of a home I want. That's the way I want to bring up my children." But it isn't easy. It costs sacrifice, it costs time and patience and love and understanding. Then the world calls. The clubs and the organizations and society invite you in. They promise you position and pleasure and pictures in the paper. You are standing now at Kadesh-Barnea. Which shall it be? The Christian home and the fine children, or the world and its pleasures and children who have lost the true meaning of life?

I was talking the other day to someone about a girl who is now faithful to her church and a Christian life. I asked the question, "Do you think that she will continue in this faithfulness when she grows up?" And the answer came back, "No, her parents are worldly, indifferent to the church and socially ambitious. We will lose this girl before long." This is a sad comment, but it is true about 99 times out of 100. When the parents turn their backs upon the Christian life at Kadesh-Barnea, the children are likely to do the same thing.

V. There Is the Kadesh - Barnea of Affliction

My father died as I sat by his bedside. I went into another room and told my brother about it. He began to weep and said, "It makes you want to be a better man, doesn't it?" I agreed that it did. Often when we lose a loved one we are so deeply impressed and so moved emotionally and so stunned by the finality of death, that we declare life will be different from that moment on. We are standing then at Kadesh-Barnea. We can go over and take our stand for the Lord, or we can go back to the same old life.

Sometime ago I visited a good man who doesn't have long to live. He has been a loyal and faithful member of our church. His son never goes to church. The son has a good job and a nice family and a beautiful home, but he never gives a penny to the church. I told this man that I hoped his son would soon come to church and take his place. He broke down and wept and said, "I would rather have that than anything else on earth." Now when that father dies his son will stand at Kadesh-Barnea. He can follow in the footsteps of his father and be a wonderful man and a faithful Christian, or he can stay in the barren land of a wasted life. I wonder which it will be. Some men hear God's voice in the hour of affliction and harden their hearts. Some hear His voice and realize that God is just reaching out to them. They cross over the line and their lives are richer than ever and God is nearer than ever.

VI. There Is the Kadesh - Barnea of a Great Prayer Life

We read about prayer, we hear about it, we know that others have received wonderful answers. Then we say, "I am going to set aside a time in my life to pray and get close to God." Then the duties of life press upon us, we get busy in the world. We choose the easy way out and our prayer life is neglected.

Hudson Taylor, the great missionary to China, was a wonderful man of prayer. One day a preacher asked a close friend of Taylor's to tell him the secret of Taylor's great life. Here was his answer. "The missionaries in China are constantly surrounded during the day by the Chinese people, so little time is given for prayer and communion with God. So to overcome this difficulty, Taylor would arise every morning at 3 o'clock, go to his room, lock the door, and spend the time until dawn on his knees in prayer or studying the Bible. Often he would sit with folded hands, looking up as if he were looking into the face of God and saying over and over again the name of Jesus."

No wonder Hudson Taylor was one of the greatest Christians the world has ever known. You can be a better Christian than you are. On one side of Kadesh-Barnea is a prayerless and barren life. On the other side there is a prayerful and a fruitful life.

VII. There Is the Kadesh - Barnea of Service

There are two kinds of people in every church. One man is content just to have his name on the roll. He does nothing for God. The other believes that he is saved to serve. Both have come to Kadesh-Barnea. One has stepped over into the land of service, the other is still out in the wilderness. Why are some Christian lives so tasteless? Is it because they are trying to get along in the Christian life by taking the easiest path? They come to church as little as possible, they are always looking for excuses. They give as little as they can, just so they will feel that they are not complete dead-beats. They never let their religion interfere with anything else they want to do.

A man in Illinois was gloriously converted. He was a man of means. He owned several thousand acres of land and many cattle. Fortune seemed to smile upon him every day. But the day he was converted he began to search his heart to see if God was pleased with his life. Later he felt that the Lord wanted him to preach. He came to his Kadesh-Barnea, his moment of decision. He finally sold out his holdings and went to school to train as a missionary. In school he devoted himself to earnest Christian service. He didn't want to lose any time so he paid the salary of a missionary to serve in his place until he could go.

Young woman, young man, are you facing your Kadesh-Barnea? God wants you to come over and give Him a life of service. The world calls you to a life of ease and pleasure. Which will it be?

I know two men who felt the call to preach in the same service. One man followed the call, turned his back upon business, went to school and for many years has served as pastor of a great church. The other man did not follow through on God's call. Today he has a small job. He wields no Christian influence. He never goes to church, he never gives a penny to the Lord. He lives between his rooming house and the office where he works. That is about the sum total of his life. At Kadesh-Barnea he said "Yes" to God, but he never crossed over.

I am afraid that some of you will say, "I want that life of blessing. I want to be good. I want to be consecrated. I want to be useful. I believe God wants me to be, but I don't want to start today. I will wait until some other time." And while you tarry in the wilderness the sands of life are running out and you are farther and farther away from the life you ought to live.

If the children of Israel had gone in they would have found sweet fellowship with God. Their communion would have been so wonderful that they could almost have seen God face to face. But they went back into the wilderness, sacrificing all the good things God had for them. This can happen to you, too.

Now these people kept other people out of the Promised Land also. Joshua and Caleb deserved to go in, but they were kept out by the failure of others. If you fail to go in and live the right kind of life, some member of your family may be kept out of heaven. Influence is a powerful and often deadly thing.

You can do one of two things when you reach Kadesh-Barnea. First, you can go back into the wilderness. This meant for Israel forty years of wanderings, fightings and failures. It could mean the same for you. It could mean an up-and-down, hot-and-cold Christian experience. It could mean a wasted life. It could mean that you would come to the end of the way empty-handed. Or by making a decision for God, it could mean a beautiful and happy Christian life and a full heaven at the end of the way.

And remember this, these people were so careful about their precious bodies, they were afraid to risk them in following God. But very shortly every one of them was in the grave. Only Caleb and Joshua got to go into the Promised Land. You are so careful about your own pleasure and comfort today, but before long your time will be up. You will be gone. Then all that counts will be what you have done for Jesus.

> Just one life,
> 'Twill soon be past
> Only what you do for Christ will last.

A rich woman owned a wealthy estate in Scotland. Suddenly she became ill and visited various places in Europe seeking to recover her health. She went to Baden-Baden, to Carlsbad and Homberg, but she got worse instead of better. Then a great physician said to her, "Medicine will not help you. There is just one chance for you. You must go and drink the waters of Pit Keathly, Scotland." "Why," said the woman, "those springs are on my own estate." She went home and drank of those waters and soon regained her health.

So men go everywhere seeking happiness and contentment when all they need to do is to cross the border into the Promised Land of a good Christian life, where they will find fellowship with Christ, sweet and enjoyable and enduring.

10.

The Clay in the Potter's Hands
(PART ONE)
Jeremiah 18:1-11

The best of men sometimes become discouraged. In the text we look in on one of the prophets of old, Jeremiah. He has been called "the weeping prophet," simply because his heart broke as he looked upon the sins of Israel. God had called him to preach and to call Israel to repentance. He did the best he could, night and day, pleading for Israel to give up her sin and return to God. But it seemed that all his efforts were in vain, for the people went on in their sin, forgetting God. Every preacher has stood where Jeremiah stood. The pastor stands before his people Sunday after Sunday, year after year. He pleads with them to leave their sins and give God the first place in their lives. He pleads with them to love each other and to be kind and gentle and Christ-like. He pleads with them to trust God and to be generous in their treatment of His church. But many of them sit and listen unmoved, then they go out to live and sin and hate just as they have been doing.

Well, God wanted to teach Jeremiah a lesson so He sent him down to the potter's house. Jeremiah went in and watched the potter at his work. That artist took up a lump of clay in his hands, then placed it upon the wheel. Then as he turned the wheel his skillful hands moulded the vessel into shape. In a moment the vessel was finished and Jeremiah must have said, "What a beautiful vessel!" But the potter frowned and said, "No, there is a flaw in it." So he crushed the vessel in his hands, put the clay back on the wheel and made a vessel that satisfied him.

94

Now here is the primary application and the lesson that Jeremiah learned. Israel had been chosen of God to be a useful vessel. But because of her sin she had failed God. God has the power to break her or make her over again, even as the potter broke the vessel. But Israel did not repent. The people went on in their sins and God had to send them away into captivity. But here is the personal application for today. God has wonderful plans for our lives, but we mar those plans by our sin and selfishness. But if we will turn away from our sins and return in penitence unto God, He can still use us. Simon Peter marred God's plan, but God made him over and he became the preacher of Pentecost. Mark marred God's plan, but God made him over and he wrote the second Gospel. Paul marred God's plan, but God made him over and he became the man who influenced the world in a way second only to Christ.

Three things we see in this story:

1. GOD HAS A PLAN FOR OUR LIVES
2. WE OFTEN MAR THOSE PLANS
3. GOD CAN MAKE OUR LIVES OVER AGAIN

I. GOD HAS A PLAN FOR OUR LIVES

1. *It is God's plan first that we recognize Him as the Sovereign and Almighty God.* So many people go along in life absolutely ignoring God. But our first responsibility is to recognize that God exists and that He is above all, and that we are subject to Him in all things. How can a man look around him and say, "There is no God"? How can a man trace the course of human history and say, "There is no God"? There is only one answer, and the Bible gives it. "The fool hath said in his heart, there is no God." So the man who doesn't recognize the existence and sovereignty of God has to classify himself as a fool.

2. *It is God's plan for us to receive His Son as our personal Saviour.* Acts 4:12, "Neither is there salvation in any other; for there is none other name under heaven given among men, whereby we must be saved." Now here is

where the whole world divides. The Bible plainly teaches that salvation is in Christ. No man is saved until he has repented of his sins and trusted Christ as his Saviour. No man is on the way to heaven unless he has had an experience with the Saviour who put him on that road. But so many people ignore the plain teaching of the Scriptures. They say that a man must do this thing or that thing or some other thing in order to be saved. They say that he must do penance or go through some form or do some good work to be saved. But listen to *Ephesians* 2:8, 9, "For by grace are ye saved through faith; and that not of yourselves; it is the gift of God; not of works, lest any man should boast."

3. *It is God's plan for us to live separated lives.* God doesn't expect from us the same kind of life after conversion that we lived before we knew the Lord. The world feels the same way. When a preacher speaks about separation the people generally think only of physical separation. They think of staying out of bars and away from questionable places. But why not think of separation of the spirit? Yes, we ought to stay out of bars, but we ought also to get all bad feeling out of our hearts. If Christ taught anything He taught love and gentleness toward others. *Ephesians* 4:32 sums it up, "And be ye kind one to another, tenderhearted, forgiving one another, even as God for Christ's sake hath forgiven you."

A woman who was a church member said that she wanted to win someone else to Christ. So one night this married woman left her husband and two children and went with another man to a saloon. She sat there drinking beer with him and trying to talk to him about salvation. You can imagine how far she got. A Christian who doesn't separate himself from worldly practices will never have any influence for Christ.

4. *It is God's plan for us to be loyal to His church.* Is it an accident that we have an institution in the world which is called the church? Did some man or group of men found it? No, it is of divine origin. Jesus Christ founded the church and He put it down here to make His Name known

to all men. As an illustration let us think of Sears, Roebuck, and Company. Their headquarters are in Chicago. But they wanted their products sold all over the world, so they put their branches in many places to carry out their plans and purposes in the world. Well, Jesus has His headquarters in heaven. He wanted His plans and purposes carried out on the earth. He wanted His Gospel preached here, so He established His church upon the earth. Our church is one branch working out from headquarters. And every true Christian wants to be a part of this church and wants to participate in its work.

Sometime ago a woman said to me, "I am a Christian and a Baptist but I will never join your church as long as there are certain people in it." I am afraid that she is going to be greatly disappointed when she gets to heaven. A young man came in my office and began to talk to me about religion and the new birth. I asked him the question, "Where is your church membership?" He replied, "Oh, I am a Christian, but I don't believe in being a member of any organized church. I am a member of the Church Universal." But if it hadn't been for the local church he never would have heard of Christ. The local church is the institution that has cradled and kept the Gospel over the years. The word for Church appears a hundred and fourteen times in the New Testament. It is used thirteen times to refer to the church as an institution. It is used ninety-six times to refer to it as a local congregation. We have nothing to do with the universal church. That is in God's hands. But we do owe an obligation to the local assembly.

I would like to ask these questions. Who is the pastor of the invisible church? Where does it hold its services? Where are its missionaries? It is God's plan for every Christian to get into a local church, to support that church with his tithes and offerings and to be faithful in all of its work.

Sir Michael Faraday was one of the world's greatest scientists. He was also a great Christian. One night a group of distinguished men came to hear him speak. By his words and demonstrations he held them spellbound as he spoke of the magnet. When he finished his lecture, the house rocked with enthusiastic applause. Then the Prince of Wales, who was present, proposed a motion of congratulation and thanks to Faraday. This motion carried amid renewed thunders of applause. Then the crowd waited for Faraday's reply. They looked around, but he was gone. It was prayer meeting time in his church and he had slipped away during the applause. He had gone out to renew fellowship with God and his Christian friends. Yet many church members have never been to a Wednesday night service. But it is God's plan for us to be loyal to His church.

5. *It is God's plan for us to live like Jesus.* We will never live in a house like the one He lived in. We will never travel as He did. We will never perform the miracles that He did. But we can still have His spirit and live in such a way that others will see Jesus in us. It was said of the Apostles, "They have been with Jesus." They didn't say this because of their looks, because of the clothes that they wore or the language that they used. They said it because they lived consecrated Christian lives. They said it because the Apostles were different from the world in every way.

A great English preacher tells of how, in his younger days, he had a good church but he was not happy. He just kept going through the motions. Then he met another preacher who was buoyant, happy and successful. "What is the difference between me and you?" he asked the second preacher. "You seem so happy and I am in the trough of the waves." The other preacher said, "There is nothing that I have that you can't have. Have you given yourself up entirely to Christ?" The preacher said that he winced because there was one point where he had not made a full surrender. He went to his room and fell upon his knees. He said that he gave God the keys to every room in his heart except one little closet. Then God said to him, "Are all the keys here?" And he answered, "All but one. It is the key to just one little closet, God, I want to keep a certain thing in it." Then God put the keys back in his hand and said, "If you cannot trust Me with all, you do not trust Me at all." The Lord started to go away and the man cried out, "Wait, O Lord, take the key, take all of me." In a little while God had cleaned out that closet and from that time on the ministry of this man was marked with great success and power.

Listen to me, you have given up many things for Christ. Is there still some little something which is still unsurrendered? Are you holding out on God? Maybe it is a secret sin. Maybe it is a hot temper. Maybe it is a mean disposition. Maybe it is covetousness. Oh, whatever it is, give it up. Only then can your life be filled with peace and power.

6. *It is God's plan for us to serve Him.* He has served you, hasn't He? He gave His Son for you, He saved you, He has blessed you all along the way. He has cared for you and He is taking you to heaven. The relationship ought not to be one-sided. As He has served you, so ought you to serve Him.

One of the tragic things of modern life is the terrible lack of a sense of responsibility on the part of many people. The business men of today tell you that their biggest problem is to get their employees to see the needs around them and to assume individual responsibility. And it is even worse in the Lord's work. The average church member is content to let someone else do all the work. He believes that we ought to have a Sunday school in which to teach the Bible, but don't ask him to teach in it. He believes that we ought to have activities for the young people, but don't ask him to help in this work. He believes that we ought to have a good choir, but he doesn't want to give any time for rehearsals. Jesus said, "I must do the works of Him that sent me, the night cometh when no man can work." As God gave Jesus a task, so does He give one to you and me. Do not say, "Tomorrow or next week or next year." The night of death may come and find your work undone.

I believe with all my soul that I found God's plan for my life on a June morning in Athens, Georgia, many years ago. I went to work in Atlanta when I was sixteen. Six years later I had had about nine jobs. I didn't stay long at each place. Some of these changes came about as promotions, but as a whole, they came about because of a restlessness of spirit. I had not fitted into God's plan. I had not found His will for my life. But on that June morning God spoke to me. I believe that He spoke to me just as surely as He did to Abraham or Noah or Paul. He told me that He wanted me to preach the Gospel. Now the years have gone by and I have never wanted to walk any other road. I shudder when I think of what life would have been for me if I hadn't answered His call that morning. I have not done as well as I could have done. I know that at least on one occasion I went to Tarshish when He wanted me to go to Nineveh. Yet there is no doubt in my mind that it was God's plan for me to serve Him as a gospel preacher.

> I had walked life's way with an easy tread,
> Had followed where comforts and pleasures led,
> Until one day in a quiet place
> I met my Master face to face.
>
> With station and rank and wealth for a goal,
> Much thought for the body, but none for the soul,
> I had entered to win in life's mad race
> When I met my Master face to face.
>
> I had built my castles and reared them high,
> Till their towers pierced the blue of the sky,
> I had sworn to rule with an iron mace
> When I met my Master face to face.
>
> I met Him and knew Him and blushed to see
> That His eyes, filled with sorrow, were fixed on me,
> And I faltered and fell at His feet that day,
> While my castles melted and vanished away.
>
> Melted and vanished and in their place
> Naught else could I see but the Master's face,
> And I cried aloud, "Oh, make me meet
> To follow the steps of Thy wounded feet."

My thought is now for the souls of men,
I have lost my life to find it again,
E'er since one day in a quiet place
I met my Master face to face.

So here is God's plan for your life. He wants you to recognize Him as sovereign God, to receive Him as your personal Saviour, to live a separated life, to be loyal to His church, to live like Jesus, and to serve God faithfully.

7. *These are God's earthly plans for your life, but He also has some heavenly plans for you.* First, He plans to take you out of this world and take you up to be with Him. Now this may come about in one of two ways. If Jesus comes in your lifetime God will take you up to heaven without your going through the experience of death. But if Jesus tarries some day soon you are going to die and you will have to go to heaven by that route. I say "soon" because not one of us will be here many years longer. We don't know what awaits us as we act out our little drama on the stage of life. Out there in the wings a heart attack may be awaiting us, or cancer, or a fatal accident. We don't know what the future holds, but if Christ is our Saviour, we are ready for it.

Then it is God's heavenly plan to change us. We are going to be changed in a twinkling of an eye and we will be made like unto Jesus. This old body will be made whole, it will never suffer again. This brain will be renewed in mental perfection. This spirit will be made completely Christlike. Yes, thank God, He is going to change us.

Then it is God's plan to reward us. Isn't it enough that God is going to change us and take us to heaven? We don't even deserve that, but God is so gracious and extravagant in His love that He is going to give us an extra reward for our service to Him and His church.

In the next sermon we will go further into this story and try to bring some thoughts that will bless your heart. Yes, God has a plan for our lives. One day we are going to cross over the river and stand in His presence. Then He will say to us, "Here is the original plan I had for your life."

Then He will bring out the picture of our lives as we actually lived them down here. As we look at these two pictures I hope that He can say that the lives we lived did in some measure correspond to the divine plan, and I hope that He can say in that day, "Well done, thou good and faithful servant."

11.

The Clay in the Potter's Hands
(PART TWO)
Jeremiah 18:1-11

The last sermon was based on this same text. Do you remember the story? God sent Jeremiah down to the potter's house, where he watched the potter put a lump of clay on the wheel. But the vessel that he made did not please the potter, so he crushed the clay and made another vessel. We saw three things in the story.

    1. GOD HAS A PLAN FOR EVERY LIFE

    2. WE OFTEN MAR THESE PLANS

    3. BUT GOD CAN MAKE US OVER AGAIN

Now here is God's plan for our lives, as we found in our last sermon. We are to recognize Him as sovereign God, we are to receive His Son as our personal Saviour, we are to live separated lives, we are to be loyal to His church, we are to try to be like Jesus and we are to serve Him. Now we come to the second point.

II. WE OFTEN MAR GOD'S PLAN FOR OUR LIVES

Look at the potter again. The first vessel had a flaw in it, so he made it over again. And we often mar God's plans by the flaws in our lives. Look at that drunkard reeling down the street, look at that thief behind prison bars, look at that murderer on the way to the electric chair. It is easy to see that they have ruined God's plans for their lives. But they are not the only ones. Some of us who are Christians and church members are living pretty good lives, but we have also ruined His plan. I may be writing to one now whose life could be counting for God, but God's plan for you has been ruined in some way.

1. *We mar God's plan through sin.* Adam and Eve were placed in the most beautiful garden this world has ever seen. There was no sin there. There was no sin in their lives. But one day they opened their hearts to sin and since that day all of God's world has been stained and marred. Even the physical world has been marred. After sin came into the world God said that thorns and thistles would grow on every side and man would have a hard time digging his living out of the ground by the sweat of his brow.

Now the prophecies of the Bible tell that the day is coming when all of earth's beauty will be restored and even the desert will rejoice and blossom like a rose. But until that day we must remember that even the physical world has been marred by sin.

Human society has been marred by sin. Compare Adam in the garden and that drunken bum on skid row. Compare the purity of Eve with the life of a prostitute and you will see how sin has marred human society. Why, even our bodies are marred. Disease sets its hold upon every organ of the body. And we must remember that sin is the thing which brought disease and death into the world.

Rembrandt was one of the world's most gifted painters. A portrait he painted would be worth a hundred thousand dollars today. But if you want to see how sin ruins a man you must look at the portraits he painted of himself. In the first portrait he is a handsome young man and you can see strength and character in every line of his face. You know that he is a man of great genius and promise. In the following twenty years he went through the whole catalog of human sin, then he painted another portrait of himself. The latest portrait shows shrunken cheeks, a weak chin and dull eyes. There is little resemblance to the man of twenty years before. And any man who lives for sin mars the plan that God has for him.

You can go to certain parts of our city and you can find homes that once were the pride of some wealthy owner. Formerly they were beautifully kept, they were filled with the finest furniture, at night these homes were a blaze of lights as the elite of the city met there. But the years have gone by and the former owners have died. Now those houses are empty. The spider webs are over the door. The weeds have grown up in the once-beautiful garden and the houses are rotting away. Ah, that is the picture of man's soul. Once he was destined for glory and beauty and usefulness, but he ruined the plan by sin.

I am thinking now of a young man who was a fine baseball player. He had the ability to make the big leagues. He was on the way up. While he was playing for a team in one of the minor leagues the big league scouts looked him over and were ready to sign him up. He could have been a great star, he could have made lots of money. But he never made it. He started drinking and before long he was out of baseball. Now God wants you in the big league of life. He wants you to use your talents for the glory of God and the benefit of others. But when you let sin and worldliness fill your life, the plan is ruined. Oh, how many people have started out with great promise. They could have gone to the top, but they let sin come in and ruin the plan.

2. *We mar God's plan through disobedience.* Some years ago a young man was in one of our southern colleges studying for the ministry. He fell in love with a beautiful but worldly girl. When he proposed to her she consented to marry him, but demanded that he give up his plans for the ministry. He was so infatuated with her that he turned his back upon God's call and they were married. The last that his friends heard of him he was holding down a small job in a small town. His wife had died and his children were out in the world, breaking his heart. He said that he was

the most miserable man in the world. God had a plan for him, but he ruined it through disobedience.

Back in the Old Testament we meet a man by the name of Saul. He was a big handsome fellow. He had great promise. God had some wonderful plans for him, so he made him king of Israel. He could have been known over the years as one of the world's greatest kings. But he disobeyed God, he played the fool and came to a pathetic end. To resist God is always to rob ourselves. No man ever turns his back upon God's will but that he cheats himself of the usefulness and joy which God had planned for him.

3. *We mar God's plan through covetousness.* I see Jesus and His disciples walking down the road. Oh, what a privilege they had. They walked and talked with the Divine Son of God. They witnessed His mighty miracles, they heard His great sermons, they felt the impact of His great spirit. Who is that man who serves as treasurer of the group? It is Judas. He is efficient and capable. Surely he will do great things for God. Some day he will be a mighty preacher like Peter or Paul. But alas, one day we see him lying dead in a garden. He had committed suicide. Why? Why? It was because he broke God's plan through covetousness. He sold Jesus out for thirty pieces of silver. I know men now who have money. God has given them ability to earn great sums. Now God wants them to use this money for His cause upon the earth. But they hold on to their money or use it for selfish ends. Thus the plan is ruined.

A man visited Niagara Falls and went down into "the cave of the winds." This is a place behind the falls where you can stand in a cleft of the rock and look out upon the tumbling waters. The noise is absolutely deafening. This man asked the guide how he stood such noise. And the man replied, "I never hear it." "What do you mean?" And the guide said, "When I first started to work here I couldn't stand the noise. But now I am used to it and I never hear it." Did you know that a man can get so used to the clank of gold and the ring of silver that he can't hear God's voice as once he did? Many a man has marred God's plan for him because of his love for money.

It may be that there is someone listening to me who has never trusted Christ. You have heard sermon after sermon and song after song. But the story of Christ's redeeming love is an old story. Your ears have become dulled. You never apply the truth to yourself. Oh, may God wake you up and cause you to hear His voice saying to you, "He that believeth on the Son is not condemned, but he that believeth not is condemned already, because he hath not believed in the Name of the Only Begotten Son of God." Oh, condemned man, God planned your salvation. Christ completed the plan when He died on Calvary and the Holy Spirit has spoken to your heart. If you go on in sin and without Christ, and land in hell, you will remember that it was not what God had planned for you. Don't mar God's plan through sin, disobedience, covetousness or any other evil thing.

4. *We mar God's plan by our failure to do our best for Christ.* God wants to save every man in the world, but that doesn't mean that salvation is merely a fire-escape to save us from hell. He wants us to be useful. He wants us to be good and faithful servants. I am sure that many Christians are little pop-guns for God when He planned for them to be mighty cannons. Many men are tooting tin whistles for God when they ought to be playing great organs. Many men are serving as wheelbarrows for God when they ought to be huge trucks. His plan is marred when we fail to do our best for Christ.

Often in the great crises of life we fail God because we misuse these hours. Let some great sorrow come and we grumble and complain and cry out, "Why did this happen to me?" And right then we are bearing false witness as to the power of Christianity. Oh, under all circumstances we should say, "Though He slay me, yet will I trust Him." At all times we should let the world know that the grace of God is sufficient for every hour of need.

We mar God's plan when we fail to do our best. I am thinking now of a certain judge. He was reared in a preacher's home, he went to a Christian school and graduated with honors. He had tremendous ability, but he failed to use his talents for God. He was lazy as far as the Christian life was concerned. He could have taught a Bible class of men, in fact he was given such a class at one time but in a month's time he gave it up. He could have been a power for Christ in the community, but he marred God's plan by failing to do his best.

A man who was a collector of choice china was being shown through a pottery where the most beautiful china was on display. He picked up a lovely cup and from the knowledge of the value of such things he said, "This must be a very expensive cup." But the guide said, "You can buy it for fifty cents." "Surely it is worth more than that," said the man. Then the guide said, "It was intended to be worth a great deal more, but there is a flaw in it." "I don't see any flaw," said the man. And the guide replied, "But our master does, and he will not send it out if it is not perfect." Oh, the world may look at some of us and compliment us, but our great Master, the Lord Jesus Christ, sees the flaws. He knows that we have often marred the plan by not giving Him our best.

But though we are not all that we ought to be, we can thank God that Jesus is perfect. And in perfect love He says to you and me, "You have failed Me, but some of life is still left. If you come unto Me, I will make your life over again."

Dr. Truett tells of a talk that he had with a man who was in dire distress. Because of sinful habits the man had gone down into the depths of sin. The great preacher asked him, "If you could see Christ face to face and talk with Him now, what would you ask Him to do for you?" The man quickly replied, "Sir, I would ask Him to make me over again." And that is exactly what Christ wants to do for all who have fallen short.

In the first sermon from this text we discussed God's plan for your life. In this sermon I have told how you can mar this plan. But the best is yet to come. In the next sermon I will tell you how God can make you over again. But now I can close this sermon and emphasize that God loves you in spite of all your flaws and He is just waiting to take you back in His arms and give you a new start.

12.

The Clay in the Potter's Hands
(PART THREE)
Jeremiah 18:1-11

This is the third and final sermon about the potter and the clay. Let me refresh your memory. God sent Jeremiah down to the potter's house to teach him a lesson. He watched the potter take up the lump of clay and work with it on the wheel. The vessel that he made did not please him, so he crushed it in his hand, put the clay back on the wheel and made a vessel which did please him.

Now these are the practical applications in the story for our lives:

1. GOD HAS A PLAN FOR EVERY LIFE
2. WE OFTEN MAR THESE PLANS
3. BUT GOD CAN MAKE US OVER AGAIN

In the first sermon I told you of God's plan for our lives. We are to recognize Him as sovereign God, we are to receive His Son as our Saviour, we are to live separated lives, we are to be loyal to His church, we are to try to live like Jesus and we are to serve Him. Yes, this is God's plan for our lives. In the second sermon I told you how we often ruined the plan through our sin and disobedience, our covetousness and our failure to do our best.

But here is the most glorious truth in the story of the potter and the clay. After all our faults and failures, God will make us over again if we repent of our shortcomings and give Him a chance. This truth came down from heaven. Men speak of the survival of the fittest, but Jesus comes with a glorious offer to the unfit. He is always a God of another chance. He says to us, "Do not despair, I will give you another chance." Hear God as He says, "Where sin did abound, grace doth much more abound." Hear Him as He says, "And I will restore to you the years that the locust hath eaten." Hear Him as He says, "Come now and let us reason together, and though your sins be as scarlet, they shall be as white as snow."

The third truth is this —

III. God Can Make Us Over Again

However, we must remember that before the potter made the second vessel, he had to crush it first. So God must often break us before He can make us. One of our favorite gospel songs is, "What a Friend We Have in Jesus." How did the author come to write this song? His bride-to-be died, his heart was broken, and out of that sorrow he came to know that Jesus was the best Friend anyone could ever have. Another song is, "Oh, Love That Wilt Not Let Me Go." The author of that song was engaged to a beautiful girl. He had some trouble with his eyes and when he went to the doctor for an examination he was told that he would soon lose his eyesight. He staggered out of the doctor's office a broken man. But he knew where he would find comfort. His sweetheart would sympathize with him. But when he told her his story, she said, "I will not marry a blind man." And out of the depths of sorrow he wrote about a greater love, a love that would never let him go.

The heart is never at its best until it has been broken. I have recently met some cocky young preachers. They are sitting on top of the world. They have all the answers. They have never been through the hardships and troubles some older men have endured. They could never minister to broken hearts in the most effective way until their own hearts have been broken. When that time comes, they will be driven to their knees in tears and they will become better servants of God.

A young preacher went to a funeral with an older preacher and heard the older man speak gentle words of comfort and grace. After the service the young preacher said, "I wish I could help people like you do." And the old man said, "When your heart has been broken, you will be able to help them." The young preacher had a beautiful wife and baby. He lived in a nice home and drove a good car. He had never suffered. He had never made any sacrifice. But six months later sorrow came. The precious little baby died. In the depths of his sorrow he came to have a fresh touch with God and from that time on he could render a better service to his people.

Where did Bunyan get the strength to write *Pilgrim's Progress?* It came to him while he was alone with God in the darkness of Bedford jail. The greatest sermons ever preached, the greatest songs ever written, the greatest books ever penned came from people who had gone down into the valleys and had felt there the touch of God.

After spending fifty years in Burma, many of them in prison, Adoniram Judson returned to Boston. A crowd of ten thousand people gathered to hear him. He was so weak from his trials that he had to be carried to the platform. He couldn't stand up to speak, he had to sit in a chair. The people saw his lips moving, but they could hardly hear his words. The crowd began to weep and that day twenty-one young people came forward to say, "We will go to Burma and take his place." God had broken him and God had made a blessing of him.

During the World War there lived in New York City the wife of a wealthy lawyer. Life for her was one unending quest for pleasure. Then the word came that her only son had been killed overseas. Suddenly heaven became real to her and Christ became very precious. She abandoned the old life and gave her time and wealth to the dissemination of gospel tracts to others who had been bereaved in the war. She had been broken and God had made her over again.

Now let me ask you a question. You are giving your life to

the things of this world. Christ has a tiny place in your heart. Why wait until God has to chastise you before yielding to Him and doing His will? Look in the Bible to see how God made men over. There was Samson, big and strong. God wanted him to be a great judge in Israel. But Samson, though strong in body, was weak in morals. He went to see Delilah and flirted with Satan. The time came when he was captured and his eyes gouged out by a red hot iron. He was thrown in prison and there from day to day he ground at the mill, suffering in darkness. God had broken him. Then came the day when all the enemies of God gathered in the temple. When things got a little dull someone said, "Bring Samson out. Maybe he can entertain us." Samson was brought out and he requested that he be placed between the two great pillars of the temple. Putting his arms around these pillars he prayed, "Oh, Lord, give me strength that I might slay the Philistines." God gave him that strength and he brought the house down upon the enemies of the Lord. Then we read, "He slew more at his death than in his life." God had made him over again.

Now think of Simon Peter. One day he said to Jesus, "I love You with all my heart. Before anyone can get to You they will have to kill me." Poor old boastful, impulsive Peter. Then they arrested Jesus and took Him to trial. Where was Peter now? He said he would die before permitting any harm to come to Jesus. Where was he? Standing up for Christ? No, he was out yonder warming his hands by the enemy's fire, cursing and saying, "I never knew this Jesus." Thank God, the story doesn't end there. In a little while Jesus came out and passed by Peter. He didn't say a word, he just looked at him. But that look was filled with compassion, love and forgiveness. Jesus was on the way to the cross to die for Peter. Now we see Peter weeping his heart out as he remembers how he had denied his Lord.

The scene changes. It is fifty days later. A great crowd in Jerusalem is listening to a preacher as he pours out his heart for Christ. When he gives the invitation, three thousand people are saved. Who is that preacher? Why, it is Peter, the same man who denied Jesus. But now he has been made over and he goes on serving Christ until finally he dies for Him.

Are you suffering now? Are you having a hard time? Maybe God is just testing you and crushing you so that He can make you over into a vessel fit for His service. A young woman had been confined to her bed of suffering for many months. Her aunt, a fine Christian, kept telling her to remember that God loved her. One day the young woman cried out, "Oh Auntie, if God loves me as you say He does, why did He make me like I am?" And the wise woman answered, "He hasn't made you, He is making you now." And maybe now, by taking you through the deep waters, God is making you over that you might serve to His honor and glory.

Oh, my friend, have you sinned? Have you slipped up? Have you put everything else in life before God? Then God is saying in love, "You have failed Me, but all is not lost. Come back to Me and I will give you another chance."

One of the fiercest battles of the Civil War was fought at Kennesaw Mountain near Atlanta, Georgia. The night after the battle a young twenty-year-old captain in the Union Army lay wounded on the ground. The stretcher bearers came along, looked at him and said, "He is gone. His chest is blown open." They went away and left him in the darkness. You would never have thought that this heap of bloody misery would ever mean anything to the world. But up in Massachusetts a father and mother were praying for their boy. He had been wild. The university had knocked all the religion out of him and he was known as an atheist, but his mother and father kept praying. As the young captain lay there all night, he began to think of his parents and their faith in God. He looked up to God and told Him that if He would let him live, he would spend the rest of his life in His service. The next morning the stretcher bearers came back. They found the captain alive and took him to the hospital. He called for a chaplain and told him that he was going to be a Christian. Now what possibilities could anyone see in that wounded boy lying on the battlefield? The stretcher bearers saw none. But God laid His hand on that boy and made him over again.

And what came out of that life? Here are some of the things which came from it — Temple University in Philadelphia, three great hospitals, the education of hundreds of boys and girls with the money from a famous lecture, "Acres of Diamonds." A great Baptist church in Philadelphia came out of that life. This man wrote twenty books and thousands of souls were saved under his ministry. This young man was Russell Conwell, one of the most amazing men America has ever produced. God broke him and then made him over, a fit vessel for His service.

Now God has saved you, but that is not enough. You are gaining heaven, but that is not enough. Maybe it is not in His plans to make you a great worker, but it is His plan to make you over into the image of His Son. Yonder is a building burning down and the owner remembers that his valuable Stradivarius violin is in that building. He rushes in and rescues it. It has been damaged by the heat, so he takes it to an expert craftsman and he repairs it. Then the owner tunes it, draws the bow across the strings, and it speaks to us in beautiful music. That is a picture of salvation. Christ rescues us, He makes us over, then we are to serve Him. He is the One we need. We have sinned. We have marred God's plan. We need a Redeemer, a Restorer, a Saviour. We need someone to make us over. And He is just waiting to do that when we surrender to Him.

As Jesus sat at the Last Supper with His disciples, he told them that one of them would betray Him. All of them said, "Lord, is it I?" And we should follow that example. Lord, is it I that hasn't been living as close to Jesus as I should? Lord, is it I who have lost my first love for Thee? Lord, is it I who have turned down that place of service in the church because I was too busy with other things? Lord, is it I who is not faithful to the church? Lord, is it I who has grown cold in prayer and am indifferent to Thy

Word? Lord, is it I who take all that You give and spend it upon myself?

"Oh, Lord," let us say, "if there is anything wrong in my life, if there is anything lacking there, let me realize it now and come back to Thee in humility and repentance." The Lord is still in the repair business. He is ready to make us over and give us happiness and usefulness if we will only turn to Him.

> I've tried in vain a thousand ways,
> My fears to quell, my hopes to raise,
> And all I need, the Bible says,
>   Is Jesus.
>
> My soul is night, my heart is steel,
> I cannot see, I cannot feel:
> For light, for life I must appeal
>   To Jesus.
>
> He dies, He lives, He reigns, He pleads,
> There's love in all His words and deeds,
> All, all a guilty sinner needs
>   Is Jesus.
>
> Tho' some will mock and some will blame,
> In spite of fear, in spite of shame,
> I'll go to Him, because His Name
>   Is Jesus.